G000037429

Living With Amazing Grace

A journey through grief, healing and transformation

MELANIE MACKIE

Copyright © 2019 Melanie Mackie

All rights reserved.

ISBN: 978-1-78972-586-5

DEDICATION

This book is dedicated to our little angel Grace Rose;
thank you my darling girl for our brief time together
on earth and for everything in between.

You are forever the light in our hearts and I am so
proud to be your mother.

Always.

CONTENTS

INTRODUCTION

Our culture and the incredible advances in medical science mean it is often taken for granted that when it comes to having a healthy pregnancy and bringing a baby into this world that everything will be OK and your bouncing baby will arrive safely. However, for many parents-to-be their longed-for babies simply don't survive the first trimester. Today the statistics for early miscarriage are shocking; one in four pregnancies end in loss. And for many there never is an answer or a reason why they lost their baby. In addition to the physical loss there is devastation and trauma left behind physically, emotionally and psychologically. Our society is reasonably open and liberal and yet those who suffer a miscarriage often do so in silence and it continues to remain taboo. Considering miscarriage is so common it is distressing to find it is not a subject that is discussed openly and that there is little support available for parents going through this traumatic experience.

Knowing what I now know from my own experience and learning about those who have also suffered this heartbreaking loss, there is no doubt miscarriage is an isolating and lonely time and many don't feel able to share their loss and sadness openly with others. This is often due to fear of judgement, as if your pregnancy had only just begun how could you experience such strong feelings of loss, grief and sadness?

For some parents-to-be they may accept their loss, try again and carry on with their lives regardless. But the truth is many don't. Their trauma and suffering are often endured alone, in silence and can have a detrimental effect on their health and well-being that may be experienced immediately or take hold in the weeks, months or even years afterwards.

Towards the end of 2015 we lost our very much longed for baby, Grace Rose, during my pregnancy to a missed miscarriage, which means your baby has stopped growing or died but there are no obvious miscarriage symptoms such as bleeding or pain. This may also be referred to as a delayed miscarriage. The ultrasound scan reveals that your baby has no heartbeat, or the baby is too small for the date of the pregnancy and has stopped growing.

After we received the devastating news that Grace's heart was not beating and she had subsequently died, as well as being totally bereft I desperately needed to know what to do next? Could I grieve for a baby who hadn't even been born? Would I ever feel normal, let alone any happiness or joy again? How on earth could I move forwards and rebuild my shattered life? And where would I continue to find the inner strength to try for another baby again and again, even though the chances of bringing my own healthy baby into the world were diminishing day-by-day?

I needed help and answers, quickly. This need set me off on a quest to understand everything I could about miscarriage. I wanted to know why it still happens, what the long-term effects are and most importantly how to recover fully. As I conducted my own research it transpired that there is not a lot of help or guidance available to bereaved parents-to-be. We must find our own way forwards, alone.

The fact is women like me are traumatised by the loss of their baby, overwhelmed with a unique grief, filled with sadness and have absolutely no idea how to process or accept what happened in order to rebuild their lives. In addition to grief, we are trying to cope with the silence and judgement that surrounds us.

After you lose your baby or babies, life is not the same as before. This sad, lonely experience changes you deeply and alters your entire outlook on life, whether or not you realise it at the time. Losing your baby affects you deep in your soul and life does not go back to how it once was. When you lose your precious baby, all your hopes and dreams for your future lives together disappear too. Miscarriage means your baby is cruelly taken from you almost as soon as your pregnancy began; often without any logical reason or medical explanation. And everything may have happened to you in secrecy because you hadn't yet shared the wonderful news that you were expecting a baby with your family and friends. So why bother to tell them the tragic news afterwards?

I don't believe baby loss should be keep quiet, ignored or even buried away and deemed as just one of those things; because it isn't. Your baby means everything to you regardless of the length of your pregnancy. Therefore, if you lose your baby you need to feel it is acceptable to talk about them if you wish. When our loved ones pass away, being able to openly remember them and talk about our loss is cathartic, therefore miscarriage should be no different. Being able to share our personal experiences without judgement means we all feel less alone and the severity of grief may in some way be reduced.

Grace Rose meant and still means the world to me, every single day. As each day passes, I wonder what she would be like if she had been born into this world. Who would she look like? What kind of personality would she have? Who would she have grown up to be? But we'll never know. Each and every significant date continues to be etched into my brain. I will never forget her due date, the date we lost her, or even the date my pregnancy was confirmed. I know how old she could be and continue to feel a gaping absence in our lives where she should be. And I wonder if we'll ever be reunited again in the afterlife.

The impact and gravity of losing Grace has never left me, she will always matter to us. Her spirit remains connected with mine and I believe she will continue to live brightly in my heart and soul for the rest of my days. I am not ashamed to talk about her. But she is not physically with me. Therefore, after my miscarriage I had to find a way to cope, to continue living and accept the loss of Grace. Losing her is something I know I'll never be over but as time has passed I have learnt to accept our fate and eventually committed to living my best life for the both of us.

I knew the ideal way for me to process my miscarriage was to write. To put everything I needed to down in my journal and through my written words express what I could not articulate out loud. Writing has always given me freedom to say what I really need to say without the fear of judgment or worrying what someone else might think if they heard what was going through my mind at the time. I regularly journal, blog for my business and enjoy putting pen to paper. But this writing process has been entirely different. A more gentle healing approach for me to write as and when I felt the need without any pressure. It became transparent that it is imperative I share what is true and at times this makes for difficult or uncomfortable reading. However, this is the reality. This is why people don't feel openly able to share what really happened during and after their miscarriage as it is far from a pleasant experience. It's deeply distressing and soul destroying. But somehow the human spirit of resilience gets you through.

Whether you've experienced a miscarriage yourself or are supporting someone who has, I trust my words may help you feel less alone. Through our own loss I've connected with other angel mothers all over the world, via social media and by reading shared stories and making heartfelt connections. We have all become members of a club that we'd rather not be in. But here we are, and our strength and resilience has been tested to the core. Knowing that we are not the only ones in this club matters enormously. Because at the time when you feel it is just you, sadly I know it's not.

My intention with this book is to offer some guidance if you have lost your precious baby during your pregnancy and is intended for anyone who wants to gain a better understanding of the impact of miscarriage and how to discuss it and support someone through it. My heart and soul reach out to you with empathy and love. And I am so sorry that you too have experienced this devastating loss or in some cases several losses. Those around you, especially if they haven't experienced miscarriage or know someone close to them who has, will often have no idea what to say or do to help. Therefore it is only by us all sharing our stories and using our powerful collective voices to re-enforce the message that a miscarriage must not be shrouded in secrecy and women and men need support not silence.

However uncomfortable it is to admit that we have suffered a miscarriage they continue to happen every single day all over the world. I recognise we're all unique and it is a personal choice in how to grieve and move forward. We find our own way eventually. However, whilst researching and learning more about the impact of early miscarriage there is a recurrent theme, we all need acknowledgement that our precious babies matter. For us and for our loved ones. As every pregnancy is a potential brand-new life trying to come forth from the moment of conception, regardless if the pregnancy lasted hours, days or weeks.

Despite the vulnerability and heartache I feel, I knew I would be brave and find courage to speak out and share what so desperately needs to be shared and heard. I am the change and am willing to share our story in memory of Grace Rose. Telling our story is stepping into the path of vulnerability by opening up and speaking my truth, it feels deeply exposing. My husband and I are private people. But at the same time I feel so strongly that this is what I am meant to do now. To find some meaning when I cannot get a definitive answer as to why this happened to us. And of course to honour Grace.

There is absolutely nothing I can do to bring my precious and very much longed-for baby Grace back to me; I accept it, and however difficult this is I choose not to beat myself up about what I could have done differently. What I know I can do, is share our story, with my own journey back towards the light and trust that sharing may also light a path ahead for anyone else who finds themselves submerged with the same sad dilemma and loss. This is a journey that took me from the depths of darkness and despair and somehow remarkably transformed my perspective and outlook on myself and my life for the better.

Grace remains part of our lives and always will. Her short life and soul matter. And her legacy even more so, you'll see that within the pages of the book her voice is somehow miraculously entwined with mine. So this is how I learnt to live with our Amazing Grace, albeit on a very different path than I would ever have chosen.

CHAPTER 1

LEARN TO LET GO WITH GRACE

Having children was always in my life plan. As a young girl I would play with my dolls, I loved looking after them and proudly pushed them around in their pram. My dolls had everything they needed, including lovely knitted clothes and outfits and they even had their own bunk beds in my bedroom. I'd dress them up, feed them, put them to bed, take them out to the shops; they'd even go on holiday as they all came everywhere with me. At no stage during my early years did it occur to me that I may not ever bring my own baby into the world. As I was always the mothering type, naturally I expected to have my own children as part of my life one day. However, I didn't aspire to live a conventional life or strive for a particular type of career, instead I sought my freedom over and above settling down in one place for too long. Therefore my late teens and early twenties were spent living and working in France as well as travelling to other countries, until I met my husband.

We met through work and became firm friends first; it seemed other people could see what a great match we were before we did, and as we both became single we got together and embarked on an office romance. It wasn't long before we moved in together and I knew from the start that this was the person I wanted to have children with. We lived together for eight years and eventually I convinced him to make it official and we married when I was thirty-three.

A year after we married I left my permanent job to set up my own business and became self-employed. One of the reasons I wanted to work for myself was to have more flexibility to fit around family life. I wanted to be able to work as well as be there to take care of my future children. But life doesn't always go to plan does it?

I experienced many setbacks on my quest to become a mother. There were plenty of heartfelt conversations between my husband and me, but when I felt ready he wasn't yet ready to become a father. The clock was ticking loudly, and at the grand age of thirty-four I would soon be deemed a geriatric mother, the definition being a pregnant woman over the age of thirty-five. Or as this is now referred to as being of advanced maternal age, whereby older women and their babies face an increased risk of complications during pregnancy. Therefore I didn't have a lot of time to mess about. I had never planned to be an older mum, wanting instead to feel young, vibrant and healthy with an abundance of energy with which to enjoy and play with my children. So eventually we began to try a little harder and as time passed there were often months where my period was late. I'd experience early pregnancy signs but it would all come to nothing, my period would start with a vengeance and I'd feel disappointed and disheartened over and over again.

In the meantime, my periods got worse. Every month I'd be in a lot of pain having to take strong painkillers just to get me through the agony. I'd feel so bad that I avoided leaving the house during the days when the bleeding was severe. It wasn't long before I sought medical advice as my symptoms were so debilitating and worryingly so, especially as I wanted to have a baby. When I saw my GP I explained what was happening and she advised the only method of managing the heavy blood loss and pain would be to take a synthetic hormone, like the contraceptive pill, to alleviate the symptoms. But I wanted to have a baby, so how was this going to be a solution as this hormone would also prevent pregnancy? Clearly there was something wrong with me, however I trusted her guidance and headed home. I lost count of how many times I went back to see her; the months turned into years and still I was suffering and there was no official pregnancy. She refused to refer me to see a specialist on the NHS and insisted the only thing that could help me was hormone therapy.

Four years later I was back at the surgery, being examined for a suspected ovarian cyst. I was referred to the local hospital for an ultrasound scan where it transpired it wasn't a cyst, but fibroids. Fibroids are common, especially in women of a certain age. In most cases they don't have any impact on getting pregnant, and my GP didn't believe they were causing any issues for me. However I begged to differ; I'd been suffering for years and my husband and parents urged me to get a second opinion. Thankfully I used my husband's private health insurance policy through his work and met with a private Gynaecologist who asked me more about my medical history and conducted his own ultrasound examination. As soon as I saw the screen I knew it wasn't going to be good news. He kept taking measurements and screenshots and the serious look on his face gave it away. The fibroids in my womb were large; so large one was the size of a satsuma. Back in the consulting room the Gynaecologist discussed his own findings in more detail, and he advised surgery to remove the fibroids to increase my chances of conceiving and carrying a baby to term. In his opinion there was no doubt the fibroids were preventing me from having a successful pregnancy.

This was a massive blow, especially as I instinctively knew all was not well. I had been needlessly suffering for years thanks to my GP. I trusted her expertise over my own intuition. Fortunately she has since retired from practice because in my opinion, based on my experience she was negligent in her treatment and failed to understand the severity of my gynaecological symptoms on the long-term consequence of me becoming a mother.

After many tests everything else was normal in terms of my fertility and the consultant believed, as I did, that I had been conceiving, but the fibroids had prevented the embryos from being successfully implanted in the womb and that caused the pregnancies to fail. We knew Grace was not my first pregnancy and this was likely to be the reason why my periods were very heavy and often several weeks late.

The decision was mine; did I want to continue as I was or opt to have myomectomy surgery to remove the uterine fibroids? Regardless of whether I became pregnant, I knew I couldn't continue to suffer, as by this point my periods were negatively impacting my life to such an extent that I knew the best option had to be surgery. But I was terrified I'd wake up and my womb would have been removed completely. My Mum had to have a hysterectomy in her early forties and should that be the case for me then my chances of conceiving naturally would be over for good. Contemplating this outcome filled me with fear. Usually a myomectomy is conducted via keyhole surgery and is pretty straightforward. However the fibroids in my uterus were within the lining of my womb and the consultant was not able to remove all of them entirely. I was in surgery for several hours and with these additional complications my recovery was slower and took far longer than expected. As I approached my thirty-ninth birthday and was trying to heal, my hopes and dreams of becoming a mother anytime soon were fading rapidly.

It was a tough time, as all around me my friends and family were suddenly pregnant and having their babies. Some were even onto their second pregnancies. But there was no baby for us. And then within the space of a year my nephew and two of my nieces were all born three months apart. My sister and my sisters-in-law had all been pregnant at the same time. But still no baby for us.

I love being an auntie and my nieces and nephews are a blessing. But I was feeling really low and getting fed up with having to put on a brave face for everyone else. We didn't openly share what was going on for us at the time because at that point I had not quite given up hope that one day we would become parents. But it didn't stop the questions. People would always ask me 'when are you going to have a baby?' Like I'd forgotten we didn't have children, yet.

So many people feel it's OK to ask others whether or not they have their own children. And if not, why not? Don't you want them? Why are you leaving it so long? You'd better get a move on. I've lost count of the number of times people asked me these questions. They rarely asked my husband, always me. And it became awkward and upsetting. Especially when you are trying your best. Over time I answered more honestly. I no longer cared if they felt awkward or didn't like my answer that 'Yes I do want children, no it hasn't happened for us....yet'. The yet being the most important word. End of discussion. Conversation over. For now.

Through my work I started to meet other women who didn't have their own children either. They were childless by circumstance. Meaning they wanted their own children but for many different reasons were not mothers and experienced difficulties just like me. Some had chosen to try in vitro fertilisation (IVF), which wasn't successful, meaning they had to find a new path forward without their own children. These conversations were a revelation and I wondered what the future held for us. If I wasn't going to be a mother, then who would I be? Would my life be worth living without having children? I didn't want to dwell on it too much, but reality was beginning to force me to consider my life purpose without children. And I didn't relish this possibility at all.

As a woman it is intrusive and devalues your identity when you are childless and not through choice. We are made to feel that unless we have children our lives are meaningless. Something must be missing. You have failed in your quest to be a mother. Therefore who are you? What is your role within society? My hopes and dreams always included children, I wasn't open to plan B; in fact there wasn't one. If I never had children how would I cope? Would I ever be truly happy and content without them? The weeks and months seem to whizz by as I did a lot of soul searching. I felt isolated and desperate. I didn't want to consider an alternative way of living my life. But I continued to meet and connect with other women who also didn't have children. They seemed to be doing OK. Maybe I could be too?

Following the surgery we discussed the possibility of IVF with the consultant. He advised that we could go down that route, however as we knew that I could get pregnant naturally it may not be the ideal solution. He left it up to us to discuss and decide. Immediately I knew IVF wasn't for me. Yes of course I still wanted to become a mother, however everything had already taken its toll. I'd been through enough already physically and emotionally and felt at breaking point. Ten years had passed where I had yearned to become a mother. This desire had placed an enormous strain on us both and our relationship. I wasn't willing to put myself or my marriage under any more pressure with IVF. I understood it is gruelling, financially crippling and doesn't offer any guarantee of success. I was also demoralised with the monthly disappointment, every month hoping for a miracle, only to have my hopes dashed when my period arrived. I'd spent far too long in this negative headspace and needed to give myself a much-needed break.

My husband is without any shadow of doubt my best

friend and soul mate. There is no one I would rather be with than him. We have been blessed and have a very nice life together. We have travelled extensively, enjoy each other's company and have each other's backs. I love him implicitly. But up until this point I had always felt we were never enough without our own children. I wasn't enough either. This overwhelming desire to become a mother had been a priority and at the forefront of my mind for ten years. For my own sanity I had to reconsider that my marriage and the loving relationship I have with my husband is something to be extremely proud of. During our relationship together we have faced plenty of challenging times and remained together. We are together because we choose to be and regardless of us being parents, we are still us and that is more than enough. I realised there was plenty for me to feel joyful about and grateful for. So as I approached a significant milestone in my life, reaching the grand age of forty, I decided it was time to really celebrate, get on with living my life and stop waiting for our baby to arrive. I needed to learn how to let go a little and release the endless pressure of trying to have a baby, for a while.

CHAPTER 2

DARE TO BELIEVE IN GRACE

As I had decided to make celebrating my fortieth year on this planet a priority, I pledged to embrace the experience by doing forty new things. Instead of purchasing a new pair of black boots, I went for a red suede pair. I loved cycling on my bike as a child so my family clubbed together and bought me a gorgeous blue bike, named the Duchess, which had a very girly basket on the front for my bags or shopping, and I could cycle along looking like, I guess - a Duchess. I felt drawn to crystals and stones and bought some pieces of rose quartz to get me started. On my birthday itself we flew to Nice in France, for a weekend break. Nice is a place I have always loved but hadn't fully explored. I began life in my forties feeling a little more comfortable in my own skin; I stepped up and out of my comfort zone in more ways than one and even at work I said yes more often to speaking at events and ran more of my own workshops. Life felt a little more exciting than it had been for a while.

But despite the excitement, something continued to niggle away at me from the inside. I felt stifled and blocked with my work. I craved change and no longer felt fulfilled or that my work gave me a sense of purpose. I'd lost my sense of direction and felt someone else was in the driving seat of my life. I wondered if that there had to be more to my life than this, but what?

I was feeling generally disillusioned with the world and my life, however life has a funny way of changing when you least expect it. Especially when it brings you exactly what you have desired for a very long time, except you're no longer waiting for it to show up. There was another extra special experience to add to my ever-growing list of forty new things; pregnancy. After so many years patiently waiting and experiencing seemingly endless disappointments and heartache, I was forty years old and pregnant with our angel Grace Rose, however at the time I had absolutely no idea.

I hadn't felt myself for a while, I was so tired that I constantly wanted to go to sleep. The extreme tiredness lasted all day, and despite getting plenty of rest I still felt exhausted. And my meals started to taste appalling; odd and metallic. Fatigue and odd tasting food are both classic signs of early pregnancy. But still I didn't make the connection.

Of course I'd experienced the early pregnancy symptoms multiple times before but being pregnant had escaped my radar. As daft as it sounds, by this point it no longer occurred to me that my symptoms could be due to the fact that I was pregnant. I'd stopped the merry-go-round of religiously counting the days of my menstrual cycle. I no longer cared when or if I ovulated as I was just getting on with my life. Or so I believed.

I did not expect to be expecting, therefore I put my tiredness down to my period being imminent. I still had a rough idea of when it should start so it never crossed my mind to take a pregnancy test just in case.

Around this time I'd also been experiencing a sharp ache, low down near my groin on my left side. An ovarian cyst maybe? As my period hadn't started, after several days of this odd pain I decided to go and see my GP and get checked out. For any abdominal pain they always ask whether or not you could be pregnant, so I thought it best to buy a pregnancy test, just to rule it out before going in to see her; not thinking for one moment it would be positive.

Usually if you have any sort of inkling you could be pregnant, it is a big deal isn't it? You anxiously pee on the stick and sit and wait, eyes glued to the display until it changes. Will it be positive this time, or negative? However, this time round I felt pretty chilled out about it. There was always a possibility I could be pregnant, but highly unlikely after all this time. So I did what I had to do and left it in the bathroom whilst I made myself some lunch.

My husband was out for the day watching the rugby at Twickenham, so I ate my soup alone, tidied up the kitchen and then remembered I had a pregnancy test in the bathroom. I went back in to look at the result. And there it was. Pregnant. Positive not negative. The display clearly showing two-three weeks pregnant. I jumped out of my skin. What? Really! This couldn't be right could it? There must be something wrong with it. I ran upstairs and checked my diary. Counting the days, I was perplexed that my period was over a week late and I hadn't noticed; this was most unusual.

Crikey maybe I was pregnant? I'd love to say that I was jumping up and down in elation, but I wasn't. I felt anxious, very unsure and I desperately needed my husband to come home immediately.

After what felt like the longest afternoon with me pacing around the house anxiously waiting for him to return, he arrived home. As I greeted him, I said there was a surprise for him in the kitchen. He thought I'd bought him a nice cheesecake as a treat. He looked disappointed when I told him there was no cheesecake. I asked him to close his eyes while I placed the positive pregnancy test into his hands. He opened his eyes, looked down and his face was one of sheer and utter disbelief. I don't think he knew what to say or do. Neither did I, we just stood looking at the test and back up at each other.

Was this really happening to us now? Was our baby finally on the way to us? Would it be our turn? This was one of those life moments when everything feels surreal. Like it isn't really happening. That it might be one big joke. Except there is a small glimmer of hope because we had a positive pregnancy test in front of us. Maybe just maybe we'll be OK? Maybe everything is alright? Maybe we are going to have our own baby after all?

I couldn't celebrate; I immediately suspected something had to be wrong. I craved reassurance, I needed to be checked over properly and my pregnancy had to be made official by the doctor before I could even entertain the idea that it was really happening. For us.

The next day I spoke to a GP at the local surgery and she arranged for me to go immediately to the Early Pregnancy Unit (EPU) at the Royal Berkshire Hospital in Reading, to have an ultrasound scan to check and see what was happening. As my pregnancy was still early, around five - six weeks, this was an anxious day, waiting for what felt like forever to be seen. You sit and wait in a room with other parents-to-be and one-by-one are called through for tests and scans. Eventually, a nurse called me through to test my urine sample, check my blood pressure and go through some questions. I asked her if my pregnancy result was still positive and she said yes, it was.

We headed back to the waiting room to await seeing the doctor and the sonographer for the ultrasound scan. I really hoped we'd have some good news. It would be amazing to see our baby, however small, on the screen. Eventually the doctor called us into another room and after waffling on and on, he told us that their test result was negative and that they were not going to do the scan as they believed I wasn't pregnant.

I could not believe what I was hearing, how could I suddenly not be pregnant? Stunned by his response I offered to show him my own test result that was sitting in my bag, this clearly indicated I was pregnant only twenty-four hours before, so what had changed? Despite what the nurse had said earlier, he told me they had tested my urine again and the result was negative, not positive. He assured me their testing equipment was sophisticated and they didn't rely on over the counter tests, therefore there was nothing more they would do. He wouldn't even scan me to check whether there was a viable pregnancy or not.

We'd arrived at the unit full of hope and anticipation only to be told that there was no pregnancy and no baby. I was bewildered and stared at him in disbelief, I couldn't utter a word let alone kick up a fuss about how I believed he was the one in the wrong. Why didn't we insist they do the scan anyway, it would have only taken minutes? Why did we trust his result over and above our own? Simply because he was the doctor, doing his job. We believed at the time that he knew what he was doing and trusted he knew best. I looked at my husband and shook my head, this couldn't be right. Surely, he was wrong? With plenty of people sitting in the corridor waiting to see him, there wasn't any more to discuss. The doctor stood up, my husband thanked him for his time as we grabbed our coats, walked quickly through the waiting area, left the maternity department and headed for the car park.

Somehow I managed to hold my emotions in check until I reached the safety of our car and then I swiftly burst into tears. Yet again all my hopes had been shattered and stamped on, my dreams of becoming a mother seemed even further away and I couldn't comprehend what had just happened. Had my test result been mixed up with someone else's? There had to be a mistake or at least a logical explanation. The glimmer of hope felt only an hour before had come to absolutely nothing, again. As the tears rolled down my face my husband drove home in silence. The thoughts continued to whirl through my brain as to how in the short space of twenty-four hours had I gone from almost believing I was pregnant to suddenly not being at all?

I had all the positive signs and symptoms and a positive pregnancy test, this couldn't be my mind and body playing tricks on me pretending I was pregnant, could it?

I was so tired of this rollercoaster of emotion and the overwhelming feelings of bitter disappointment arose once more; what a familiar feeling this was to me. My heart sank. In fact my heart ached with the physical pain of overwhelming sadness.

Maybe it was time to simply accept the fact that I was not destined for motherhood in this lifetime? Maybe I should just forget all about trying for a baby? Maybe I just needed to embrace other things to help fill the gaping gap in my heart and soul? But I couldn't give up. Not yet.

Every human being has a gut instinct that tells us when something is physically wrong within our bodies. When something doesn't feel right inside, it's usually because it isn't and we know we should pay attention. We know our bodies better than anyone else, including the professional medical establishment. Several days after the latest big disappointment at the hospital, my period had still not arrived. I continued to feel unwell and experienced many of the typical symptoms and signs of early pregnancy. In addition to the extreme tiredness and horrible tasting food, I also felt uncharacteristically emotional and had sore breasts that seemed to take on a life of their own. Plus I had to pee all the time.

I frequently experience vivid dreams, so vivid and life-like that I'll instinctively know something about a person or situation. If I am deliberating on something or a situation the answer or the solution I seek tends to come to me crystal clear, especially during the early hours of the morning. So it wasn't too much of a surprise to find myself wide awake at dawn with an inner knowing; I knew without any doubt I was pregnant with our child. Despite what the doctor had told me at the hospital, I knew this to be true. I no longer doubted myself or my instincts.

After I ate some breakfast, I made my way towards the chemist and purchased another two pregnancy tests. I did the first one and immediately it came back with the positive result on the display showing two-three weeks pregnant. I waited a few hours longer before doing the second one. Yet again another positive result appeared. Maybe there was a chance I was really pregnant after all? After speaking to my husband, I called my GP to discuss what had happened and informed her of our experience at the EPU. She was annoyed that they hadn't even bothered to scan me during our initial visit as she'd requested. However, she said that pregnancy tests are usually accurate and was happy to confirm my pregnancy. She encouraged me to rest as much as possible and advised when to make arrangements to see the midwife in a few weeks' time.

We finally dared to believe that I was officially pregnant. Whilst it was fabulous news, I still didn't feel able to truly relax and celebrate. But maybe at last we were going to have a baby; our baby. The next milestone was to reach my first midwife appointment, in three weeks' time. This appointment could not have come soon enough. The countdown began.

In the UK people tend to keep their pregnancy news under wraps during the first trimester until you've had the first scan around the twelve-week mark. This is deemed to be safer. Therefore once you're in the safe zone you're officially pregnant. However this means many couples and parents-to-be who go on to experience a miscarriage, or even several, rarely tell their families and friends. If their pregnancy ended in loss, they want to avoid sharing the sad news afterwards. However, I believe you're pregnant the moment you know you're pregnant, so we took the decision to share our wonderful news with our families and those closest to us. It was still early days but it had already been a long road for us, so I felt we'd be needing more of their support and encouragement in the weeks ahead. It turned out we would need them in more ways we could ever imagine.

Eventually all the people we loved and cared about knew I was pregnant and were delighted for us. Some knew of and understood the extent of our journey, but the majority didn't. They had no idea just how difficult the journey had been to get to this point. Slowly it began to sink in that I was expecting a baby, although I continued to feel hideous and wondered how I was going to get through the next few weeks. It felt like an eternity waiting to see the midwife, so it was tentative gentle steps forward day-by-day, waiting patiently for the days to pass and I tried to keep my mind occupied elsewhere. Being self-employed meant I didn't have to do too much or leave the house to go to work so this helped me get some rest and take it easy.

We were slowly getting used to the idea that we were going to become parents, but we were not outwardly celebrating, we were fraught and on edge. I bought some cuddly toys and decided on the pram I wanted to have but that was as much shopping and planning I could allow for the time being. Having faced so many disappointments and setbacks we knew what could go wrong and so this took away the blissful happiness that many couples experience when they learn they're going to have a baby together. Despite desperately wanting to become a mother I felt daunted at what lay ahead, my emotions ranged from extreme happiness and elation one minute to a head full of worries the next. We'd been through so much and it was a lot for us both to take in and process. Neither being willing to look too far ahead into the future, just in case something went disastrously wrong.

During an online chat with my sister-in-law Nicola and her family in Australia, we joked about baby names. There were plenty of suggestions and some were better than others. We'd always had a boy's name in mind, and I was convinced at the time this baby would be a boy, although we kept this to ourselves. But if it was a girl, we really didn't know what we would call her.

Randomly one afternoon whilst working in my home office I had a moment of clarity and knowing. That our baby was a girl and her name would be Grace Rose. I didn't question it or try to push it away, so when my husband arrived home from work I shared my latest insight - the baby is a girl and she'd like to be called Grace Rose. We both smiled. Grace she is.

To back up this theory of inner knowing, I came across an old notebook whilst cleaning out a drawer in my office desk. Contained within was a post-it note listing girls' names that I liked. I had no idea how long it had been since I wrote these names down, it had to have been several years at least. Slap bang in the middle of the post-it, as clear as anything was the name 'Grace Rose'. This was even more remarkable, as I had no recollection of writing it down in the first place. A coincidence, maybe? I beg to differ.

Knowing that Grace had her own name, meant she had an identity, she wasn't just a baby she was and is Grace. Our Grace. But this wasn't the only strange incident to occur. Once we knew Grace was Grace, we both began to see the name Grace everywhere. Whilst on the train travelling into work, my husband texted me to say that there was someone directly opposite reading a book about Grace. We'd watch a programme on TV and the main character would be called Grace and I'd log on to Pinterest and see endless images and quotes all about Grace, many of which are included here within this book. There were so many seemingly random sightings and signs of Grace that we both got her message loud and clear.

Having the love and support from our families and those we trusted meant my pregnancy was not shrouded in secret. I didn't have to pretend it wasn't happening until the safety of the second trimester and it was lovely that we could get excited with them. But still I couldn't shake off the sense of anxiety.

Three long weeks eventually passed, and we headed off to the local community centre for the first midwife booking-in appointment. The midwife checked me over, briefed us on all the appointments we'd need and asked which hospital I wanted to give birth in; as long as it wasn't at the Royal Berks in Reading I was happy. After the initial experience at the EPU with the doctor telling us I wasn't pregnant, when clearly I was, being under their care didn't fill me with any confidence. So I opted to go to Frimley Park Hospital in Surrey instead and we were hoping to move out of the area therefore Frimley was ideal. Suddenly everything became very real, and due to my age and being officially labelled as a geriatric mother I was going to be under the care of a consultant and monitored very closely throughout my pregnancy. There would be plenty more tests, pre-natal appointments and scans to follow, more than you would have if you're under the age of thirty-five.

I felt a little more reassured, however, I recall feeling anxious and discussed my concerns with the midwife. I told her that I felt I couldn't relax fully or totally embrace being pregnant until I'd heard our baby's heartbeat and saw for myself on the ultrasound scan that all was well. The midwife did her best to put me at ease and suggested I focus on reaching the next significant milestone, the twelve-week scan in another three weeks. I tried to let go of my fears and relax and ease into my pregnancy; could I dare to believe in Grace?

CHAPTER 3

A PRECIOUS MOMENT WITH GRACE

Suddenly my body changed rapidly and I began to expand. My clothes felt tight and uncomfortable, but the good news was that the awful overwhelming nausea that I'd experienced for five weeks started to recede. I hoped the worst part of the first trimester of my pregnancy was over. Ready to face the world once more I left the cocoon of our home and attended a local networking meeting that I always enjoyed. Once there, it was wonderful to see some friends and familiar faces and afterwards I enjoyed having lunch with my friends. I shared my pregnancy news as it was increasingly difficult to hide my ever-expanding middle, and one of my friends had guessed I was pregnant the moment she saw me.

Finally, I relaxed a little more and embraced talking about my pregnancy. I believed that everything was progressing well and as each day passed I felt more at ease and excited about the future with our baby. Being out and about did me the world of good and I hoped to be able to go out more frequently, especially as I no longer felt the constant desire to retch. After my lovely outing I made my way back home; it had been a happy day.

That is until I got home and went to the toilet. As I wiped myself, I noticed a small amount of blood on the toilet paper. Not a lot, just a speck or two, but this was more than enough for me to panic. I texted my husband, called my Mum and rang the doctor. I tried to convince myself it was nothing to worry about. I knew that pregnant women can experience spotting and bleeding and everything could be absolutely fine, but then again maybe it wasn't? My instinct rarely failed me, despite trying my utmost to reassure myself and not panic, I knew something was drastically wrong with the baby. Something had happened. Something so precious was going to be taken away from me again. I just KNEW; and my heart sank.

My doctor called me back and advised rest and to keep as still as possible. She booked in another scan at the EPU, but they wouldn't be able to see me until the following week which only meant even more time to wait. I was on edge and spent the afternoon and evening wrapped up in a blanket lying on the sofa staring into space. I didn't dare move. My cat Lola sat with me, she sensed something was wrong and didn't leave my side. All I could do was wait for my husband to get home from work. As soon as he walked through the door I broke down into sobs in his arms. I was utterly terrified and powerless to do anything but keep anxiously waiting. Throughout my pregnancy I needed reassurance, I wanted someone to tell me that everything was going to be OK with my baby. From the moment we knew I was pregnant I hadn't been able to rest or fully relax. I am not a patient person at the best of times and like to feel I am in control of my destiny. But with pregnancy you are far from being in any sort of control, so one of my pregnant friends suggested I have a private scan at a local clinic, as she had done so, and it had eased her own fears. Fortunately, I'd booked an appointment as she had suggested, several weeks before and didn't have long to wait as we were due to go there the following morning for an ultrasound scan.

There wasn't any more blood lost overnight but neither of us slept. To add to our sombre mood a terrorist attack had occurred in Paris the night before. France is my second home and a special country to us both, so as soon as we got out of bed the day was already feeling dark, miserable and sombre. As we made our way to the clinic, I couldn't listen to the sad updates on the car radio. Instead I prayed. Inside my head I repeated my prayers and begged the powers that be to please let everything be OK today. Please let our baby be healthy. *Please. Please. Please.* Despite my prayers I knew once more in my heart and soul everything was not going to be OK. Something awful was relentlessly nagging away at me. What could it be?

We arrived at the clinic and both sat in the waiting room in silence. Every wall visible was covered in beautiful canvases featuring other people's babies and miraculous scan posters. Even the coasters on the table were of baby images. Everywhere you looked you could see picture-perfect babies; cute and smiling at us. I anticipated seeing ours too. We were called in for the scan and I lay down on the bed with a large monitor screen directly in front of us on the wall. The sonographer started by asking lots of questions and tried to put us at ease. Following the incident at the hospital when the doctor refused to scan me, I half expected to see nothing; that my pregnancy was a phantom, teasing me. The vivid dreams I'd had continued to occur where I'd be proudly pushing a pram, except every time I looked down to see my baby, there was nothing there. The pram would be empty. It always gave me chills.

We stared at the screen in anticipation. In what felt like an age later the sonographer finally located our baby. She was there, on the screen. In front of us we could see our baby. It was incredible; miraculous. A new life right in front of our eyes. Initially there was excitement between us, I hadn't imagined her after all. The sonographer said she had located our baby and was trying to find her heartbeat. Initially she said she had it and for a moment we were in awe. Time seemed to stand still for a moment, until the atmosphere suddenly changed. She was having difficulty confirming a heartbeat again. After four more attempts she uttered the devastating words; words we never ever wanted to hear, 'I am so sorry guys, this doesn't look good I cannot locate your baby's heartbeat, I believe she's gone'.

As I recall this utterly devastating moment, I remember feeling initially calm. Because I had received the news I somehow instinctively expected. As if how could things be any different? Maybe this was the shock? My husband was still holding my hand and neither of us moved an inch. We both just stared at the screen in front of us in utter disbelief. Eventually we turned and looked at each other. Our eyes met and the momentary joy we had both felt just moments before had dissipated. Now there was absolutely nothing left but immense sadness between us. Our precious baby. Our very much longed for baby. Our amazing Grace Rose. There was no heartbeat; she had gone. And in that moment I felt as if my heart had shattered into a million pieces and stop beating too.

Tragedy strikes in a moment; it can be sudden and unexpected and you wonder how life can be so cruel. How can you find yourself in a happy place surrounded with images of other people's gorgeous babies and yet suddenly learn your own baby has gone? How? And why? We'd been through so much and I failed to comprehend why had this happened to us. Surely we deserved some happiness and our baby too, didn't we? We were ushered into a separate waiting area at the back of the clinic, well away from the other excited couples awaiting their scans and positive news. To outsiders the sheer devastation must have been transparent on our heartbroken faces. As we waited, I felt anger once more with another doctor, who had told me I wasn't pregnant. Our baby had been there all along. Despite what he had told me I had known deep in my soul that our baby was there within my body. But now her spirit had left us. Our baby Grace had gone almost as quickly as she'd arrived.

The sonographer came back into the waiting area to discuss her findings and gave us an envelope which enclosed our scan images. I opened the envelope and looked at the images one by one; there was our baby; and then I completely broke down. She explained our baby had stopped growing and her heart had stopped. The official term is 'a missed miscarriage', and my body had simply failed to catch up with what had happened. With a 'missed miscarriage' all the positive signs of pregnancy remain, yet your baby is silent and still. It was time for us to leave and we made our way back to our car. Once safely inside we clung to each other again and sobbed. As my husband held me he said: 'We will try again'. With tears rolling down my face I felt it unlikely that I'd ever have enough strength to try again. I had nothing left; my heart was completely and utterly broken.

To this day I am grateful my friend suggested going to the private clinic for a scan. If I had waited for my routine scan via the NHS it would have been too late and I would have no record of Grace at all. I treasure the scan images I have of Grace; they are all safely kept within a special box along with the other precious gifts and mementos we received for her. Regardless of what anyone else believes about babies lost in early pregnancy, I know that my baby will always be remembered. Grace will always matter. She was there with me even if our time together was brutally cut short. And I have the scan images to prove it.

When we got home, we began the sad task of having to share our devastating news with our loved ones. My parents knew we were going for the scan and were expecting our call. As the day went on they'd instinctively know it would not be good news. It was even more difficult as my Mum was out for the day with her friends in London and I thought it unfair to call her to tell her directly. So I called my dad, and we had the saddest conversation of my life. My dad could not fix my sadness or total heartbreak. Our loss was their loss too. Grace was their granddaughter and my parents are fantastic grandparents, they would have been wonderful grandparents to Grace too.

My husband and I were utterly bereft. There was absolutely nothing anyone could do or say to make things feel any better, but our ordeal was far from over. The days ahead would not be any easier because despite there being no heartbeat, I was still carrying Grace. My body believed I was still pregnant, as physically I was, and it hadn't yet caught up naturally.

Another three long days passed before our next visit to the Early Pregnancy Unit, as they couldn't fit us in any sooner. This meant more waiting, anxiety and ever-increasing worries about what was ahead. Eventually we were back at the hospital again and the nurses and doctor were all kind and supportive. One of the hardest things is that those who are miscarrying must wait with those who are not. Couples came back into the waiting room along with their scan photos and smiled. They were overjoyed and beaming as they were expecting babies with heartbeats. Whilst we on the other hand were not and had to try and tune out and just wait our turn, until we could get out of there.

We made our way back into the ultrasound room and this time I did not want to see the screen. The room was silent; no-one uttered a word. The doctor eventually confirmed that our baby's heart was not beating and that a full miscarriage would be imminent. The NHS protocol at the time was not to intervene medically and to take a wait and see approach and let nature take its course. They wanted to make sure that there was no heartbeat, so I was booked in for a follow-up scan in ten days' time. I was advised that if my miscarriage started to happen physically between now and then I should see my GP or if I felt it was an emergency to contact them and go back in to be monitored. We headed home and waited for nature to take its course. Needless to say, after this scan there were no pictures of Grace to take home.

If I ever were to find myself in this situation again, I would insist they intervene immediately. But yet again you trust their judgement, follow their lead and go along with what they advise. Obviously miscarriages, like pregnancies, are unique and some may find them easier to cope with than others. I'd asked one of the nurses at the EPU what to expect when the miscarriage began and she gave me a leaflet and said that if I filled five sanitary pads in an hour then to come back in. Otherwise remain at home. Within the literature and information that I read, it referred to a miscarriage as being similar to a heavy period. A heavy period; right OK, I thought, it would be uncomfortable and maybe painful. Over the years I had experienced and coped with very heavy periods on numerous occasions, but miscarriage was something else entirely.

Later the following week, my miscarriage started in earnest and it was extremely painful, with sudden and severe blood loss which started gently and was more niggly to begin with. The pain was there, but bearable. Pain was something I felt I could cope with and I wasn't particularly alarmed at this stage. Therefore I took some painkillers and climbed into bed, knowing it was likely I'd be up again soon. Within a couple of hours the pain had increased in intensity within my lower back and suddenly I felt the blood flow surge. The cramps and contractions arrived and I leaped up out of bed rushing quickly down the stairs towards our bathroom. Once sat on the toilet, I could not move. Rooted to the spot I was shaking and my legs felt like jelly. Shouting out for my husband to help, it took a while for him to wake up and find me downstairs. As he came into the bathroom he had a look of absolute horror on his face. It was carnage. I was in so much pain and barely able to keep myself upright. I begged him to stand in front of me and hold me, but to keep absolutely still. I was in agony; contraction followed contraction as nature began to take its course. I thought I may lose consciousness and seemed to have been transported to a place outside of my body and could only hear a voice whispering 'just surrender; just surrender' coming at me from somewhere. I felt powerless to do anything else.

This wasn't a heavy period, this was a brutal, utterly terrifying, out of control nightmare. This felt to me as intense as childbirth. They hadn't told me to expect this. When would this ordeal end? It became so intense that I wondered if I'd survive the night to see another day. This trauma left me terrified, was I dying? I said to my husband 'if I make it through until morning and if I survive this, I know I will survive anything'. When I thought the worst was over, the contractions came back again and my body would shake and convulse all over again. The amount of blood loss was alarming, but not enough to be deemed an emergency. Yet. I decided that if I could avoid going to hospital I would as I had no strength and to move me or even try to attempt to sit in an accident and emergency department felt impossible. I also wanted my privacy. I did not want strangers around me as I was giving birth to what remained of our baby, this was a sacred time between me, my husband and Grace. The three of us together physically for the very last time.

Seven hours after the painful contractions began we both managed to get back into bed to try and rest. Until the contractions and blood loss started all over again. I had absolutely no choice other than to surrender to what was happening and allow my body to do what it needed to do.

Here you learn that your body is in control; you are at its mercy.

After four hellish days of miscarriage agony eventually I birthed Grace at home in our bathroom. I held what remained of our precious baby in my hands. Exhausted and utterly heartbroken, my baby and I had been together for ten weeks, but now our physical journey had come to a brutal end. Somehow, miraculously, I'd survived.

The blood loss continued and I remained in pain but it was not as bad as it had been initially so after two weeks miscarrying naturally I hoped I was over the worst. It was back to the hospital for another scan to check and see if everything had passed. But no, despite everything I'd been through there was still pregnancy tissue remaining within my uterus that had to come out. Referred to clinically as 'retained products of conception' I had enough remaining that it required removal by emergency surgery. This had been the reason for the continuous blood loss and if left untreated I'd be at risk of severe infection or sepsis. Just when it seemed I believed my physical recovery could begin, I'd hit yet another setback to knock me off my feet. The doctor explained they had to operate as soon as possible as I was at a high risk of infection and further complications and she wanted to operate later that day. But before booking me in for surgery she said she would try and remove the tissue herself. This meant even more pain and extreme agony, as well as my dignity going right out of the window. The remaining tissue could not be removed therefore the only solution was surgery.

Despite the constant pain and heavy bleeding, naively I hadn't seen this coming at all and felt totally unprepared for any surgery. I was fed up of being in the hospital and desperately wanted this ordeal to be over. I'd been through so much; my body and soul were screaming in pain. This had to stop. I panicked and wanted to run. To escape. To get away from all of it. But I desperately wanted to feel better and be free from the agonising pain. So the doctor left us alone and tried to add my name to the emergency surgery list. But there were no available beds, they couldn't operate on me until the following Monday, therefore once more we were sent home and advised to come back in immediately if I got worse over the weekend.

Whilst my ordeal was still not over, this gave me a little more time to prepare myself mentally for the surgery and rest some more at home. I sat in front of the TV watching Strictly Come Dancing and for a very short period of time normality crept back in. I've since come to realise that little moments of joy help you feel more able to put one foot in front of the other and get you through the incredible dark moments and horrible imminent procedures that are at the forefront of your mind.

Monday, the day of surgery arrived, and I'd barely slept. I still felt very anxious and panicky. I hated being in confined spaces and this terror was getting worse. I had to keep reminding myself that I'd survived the trauma of the last couple of weeks, now I could face anything thrown at me. My worst nightmare had happened; somehow I had survived and I was still here. Alive. Though not kicking yet. We'd hoped to be back at home by lunchtime, having arrived at the hospital early. They'd ushered us into a side room to wait for a bed to become available on the ward. I spent the day waiting with another lady who had also lost her baby, her fourth. I felt so much empathy for her bravery and so sorry for her losses and we chatted when we both felt up to talking. This was the first time in weeks that I didn't feel quite as alone. Someone else was also going through their own loss too. Someone else understood what I felt, and I completely understood her.

I seemed to spend all day waiting, I frantically paced up and down the corridors as I couldn't keep still lying in bed. But I had to once they gave me the pre-meds. Eventually my nerves got the better of me and I cried and cried. The doctor held me in a tight embrace and her compassion and empathy demonstrated she understood my anguish. In fact all of the staff at the hospital were kind and understanding; they offered supportive words and I appreciated them looking after me. Things like this really do matter. Sadly they see couples just like us every single day. Baby loss happens, more than we'd like to think about. And not every person is as fortunate as we were in receiving some much-needed tender loving care.

After eight hours waiting for this part of my ordeal to be over an orderly wheeled me down to theatre in a wheelchair. I had no strength left to walk by myself. Whilst being prepped for the anaesthetic, it transpired the surgeon operating on me would be the same consultant who operated on me before to remove my fibroids. It was reassuring to see him and we had a brief chat whilst they prepared me for surgery. He told me how sorry he was to see me there after everything I'd been through. I said: 'me too'.

With the surgery complete I awoke in the recovery room. My ward neighbour was in the recovery bay next to me and was just coming round too. As I looked over at her I felt such immense sadness for us both. Who knows if we'll ever get to hold our own babies in our arms?

When back on the ward I had some tea and toast and finally after weeks of experiencing intense pain it had ceased. I smiled for the first time in weeks and desperately wanted to get home and cuddle my cats, Billy and Lola, as soon as possible. I'd had enough of doctors, hospitals, tests, scans and being prodded and poked. And more than enough of the disappointment and heartache of losing my baby and wondered - is this ordeal finally over?

Depending on the circumstances of miscarriage, surgery is seen as a last resort. Our bodies know instinctively what to do and we'd all prefer to avoid any unnecessary intervention, however having spent close to three weeks miscarrying, the ordeal and trauma only served to cause me more harm physically and emotionally. My body was totally depleted and if I'd known that the severity of blood loss and the remaining tissue were a risk to my own life at the outset, I would have disregarded the medical establishments advice to wait and see and insisted on surgery immediately. We have to be better informed of the physical implications and risks of miscarriage, as it is far from a heavy, uncomfortable period; it can be life-threatening.

With the physical side of things resolved I hadn't envisaged that with this sad ending there could ever be the beginning of something else; a new spiritual path with Grace. As despite her having gone, I felt her presence around me and knew in my heart and soul she hadn't really gone anywhere.

In addition to this there was something else on my mind, by miscarrying naturally it meant I gave birth to Grace. No one could take this experience away, it had happened. Despite our brief time together, she had existed within my body. Our precious time together could not be ignored or denied by me or anyone else. She was my baby therefore did this now make me a mother, only a mother without her baby living in this world.

I didn't yet feel bold enough to claim the mother title and naively believed that once I left the hospital life would go back to normal and revert to how it was before I became pregnant. But this traumatic experience hadn't finished with me yet, it was far from over and I was about to find out how it had affected my entire being, body, mind and soul.

CHAPTER 4

SURRENDER TO THE GUIDANCE OF GRACE

Whilst at the EPU everyone who dealt with us was kind and extremely supportive, treating our loss with respect and us with dignity. But when I left the hospital the support ended, with the only advice given to wait at least six weeks for my body to heal and recover before trying to become pregnant again. Try again? I couldn't contemplate trying again for the foreseeable future. When back at home I made a phone call to my midwife and left her a message to say that I wouldn't be attending our second antenatal appointment due to the fact that I had suffered a miscarriage. She never called me back and there was no follow up. Absolutely nothing. If I wanted to talk to anyone or receive counselling then I'd have to source this assistance myself. I couldn't be bothered; talking was not going to bring my baby back to me.

Despite the lack of aftercare, I had believed the worst of my ordeal was over and I'd pick up where I left off and carry on with life as before. Except it didn't; as eventually the intense trauma and pent-up emotion had to be released and it hit me hard, like a ton of bricks. I couldn't control my emotions at all. One day I cried non-stop, the tears rolled down my face as everything rose to the surface. All I could do was surrender once more and allow the tidal wave of emotion to rise and wash over me. This was the beginning of the long drawn-out process of grieving for Grace. In addition to the grief and overwhelming feeling of loss, my hormones were all over the place. When I'd gone in for the surgery my levels of the pregnancy hormone HCG were still high and the doctor advised that it could take several weeks for them to revert to normal. In addition to my fluctuating hormones my body had been hit with the impact of a general anaesthetic, so was it any wonder I felt overly emotional, totally depleted, disorientated and experienced a complete emotional meltdown?

My mind couldn't begin to reconcile what had happened, my body felt battered and bruised and my spirit seemed to have diminished. I had experienced low points in my life before, but this was the lowest of the low. I'd never felt so totally out of control of myself and my entire life and I wondered 'what on earth do I do now?'.

I hadn't understood or realised that many miscarriages are not done and dusted in a matter of hours, until I experienced my own. In my case it had been a traumatic three weeks. For all intents and purposes I had been pregnant for thirteen weeks and everything had taken its toll on my mind, body and soul. I was shell-shocked, so how could I, in fact how could anyone, just put all this trauma aside and carry on as though nothing had happened at all?

I desperately needed answers, so I sought help and guidance. I wanted to find advice that would resonate, as every piece of information received from the hospital only focused on facts and procedures. Nothing mentioned emotional healing or how to aid recovery from a more holistic point of view. This left me feeling even more frustrated and alone; surely I was not the only woman in the world to experience an awful miscarriage and struggle afterwards.

I knew deep within my entire being just how much this pregnancy meant to me. My senses and instincts were telling me loud and clear that something major had happened. And yet I felt that because miscarriage is so common and 'just one of those things' I should be able to accept what had happened and get on with my life once more, just like everyone else seemed to be doing. Despite any logical thinking, I could not move past the fact that I had been elated to be pregnant and then utterly devastated to suddenly not be. This pregnancy and this baby meant everything to us. All our hopes and dreams had been cruelly taken from us. How could I ignore or even try to suppress and deny the depths of despair and grief I felt about this?

What doesn't help is that we have been conditioned within our western society, particularly in the UK, to wait until the perceived safety of the second trimester before announcing our pregnancies to the world. But we don't suddenly become officially pregnant only when we've had a twelve-week scan. We are pregnant right from the moment of conception. During the first twelve weeks of pregnancy our bodies go through significant physical changes and hormonal shifts as our precious babies are developing in the womb. If you were to carry a rucksack strapped to your back for thirteen weeks, you'd soon know about it. You wouldn't be able to ignore it and pretend it isn't there or happening. You'd get used to carrying it. So why is early pregnancy any different? For some reason we have been taught to keep quiet about miscarriage if it happens.

Within my own world, it was as if a grenade had been thrown at me and exploded and I was stunned. The last thirteen weeks hadn't all been for nothing. I'd spent the last three months connecting with the spirit of my baby Grace, excitedly anticipating her arrival. From the very moment I knew I was pregnant this connection was instinctive, heartfelt and instant. Therefore our loss was not something

I could bury or ignore and even put a brave face on, even if I had wanted to. My pain and anguish would not be pushed away or suppressed. I was one angry, heartbroken woman. I felt totally alone in my grief because there was absolutely no one who had this bond and deep connection with my baby, like I did. But I wasn't supposed to feel this way, was I?

Regardless of our rational minds, we are not machines. We are human beings; we are women with emotions, built-in natural instincts and deep intuition. I quickly came to realise that my overwhelming feelings of loss and grief were perfectly natural. This was the natural order of life and loss. No matter how long we are pregnant for, we carry our babies within our wombs and have an instant connection and protective bond. Yet, I couldn't protect mine. Nor could I keep her safe. Had I in some way failed her? Did I do something wrong?

Baby loss is a grief like no other, as a mother you are likely to forge a deep bond with your baby long before they are born, therefore no one else shares the special relationship you have during pregnancy. You'd spent the last three months getting used to the idea of becoming a mother and bonded with your unborn baby, and then it's unexpectedly taken from you. On top of this heartache you find yourself having to cope with some people who believe miscarriage is nothing and judge you for the intensity of your feelings. As why would you grieve for a baby who was yet to be born?

Mentioning miscarriage makes other people feel uncomfortable and they'd prefer it if you just got on with it and didn't make any kind of fuss. Some of the comments that came our way included 'oh no why have they named the baby who wasn't really a baby?' or 'so-and-so has had several miscarriages and she's perfectly fine about it all' or 'it wasn't meant to be, maybe you'll have better luck next time' or 'Oh wow you knew you were having a girl how did you know?'. (Just for the record we were never officially told we were having a girl – we believed her to be so and that was that.) Or even 'don't cry or get upset just move on and try again'.

There are many ways to support loved ones through the aftermath of miscarriage but belittling, ignoring or trying to deny their legitimate grief and how they feel is not one of them.

One of my friends said she could see how my miscarriage had totally floored me, that it had taken the wind out of my sails and had left me a broken woman. She was absolutely right in her perception. Because after my miscarriage I had many dark days and I felt utterly despondent. So despondent that it frightened me and I didn't know if I could recover or feel any joy or happiness again. Once again, I had to surrender to the grief and feel the total impact of the trauma. I couldn't avoid it therefore it hit me hard, head on.

I was at a loss and wondered what to do with myself; my husband couldn't take any more time off work, so life had to return to some sort of normal. We were in the midst of winter and the dark December days matched my mood. I didn't feel ready to go outside or leave the house alone. I didn't want to talk to anyone, I had no interest in doing anything and had little energy to see me through the day. My parents visited when they could, but not living on our doorstep meant I had to get used to being at home alone again. Physically I began to recover; emotionally I began to descend lower and lower. I was not in a good place.

Being self-employed meant I could stay at home and try to recover. I didn't have the added pressure of going into a place of work, as clearly I was in no fit state to go anywhere. I felt numb, but I was just about functioning day-to-day simply going through the motions of getting myself out of bed and dressed, but I was dazed and confused. I'd lost myself as well as losing Grace and the whole experience had rocked my entire being. I didn't want to be in this world without her. I wanted the pain and anguish to leave me alone. I just wanted to feel better. But how could I possibly feel any better? I couldn't bring her back to me. I couldn't turn back the clock. I couldn't do anything differently. And I was a long way from accepting what had happened.

Searching on how to recover from miscarriage online led me to the baby charity Tommy's. They had launched a brand new #miscourage campaign the weekend we lost Grace. This campaign focused on publishing blog posts filled with stories of baby loss to highlight and raise awareness on the impact of miscarriage.

These posts and stories became a lifeline; suddenly I realised I was not the only woman to lose her baby, there were others. Whilst still firmly in the depths of despair and darkness I read one post that resonated at precisely the right moment in time. The author had shared her own story of her miscarriage and talked in-depth about the deep fog of her grief and awful depression afterwards. She'd reached the lowest of the low, the point where she knew she couldn't go any lower. She realised she had to make a choice; would she allow herself to sink even further into the darkness than what she believed was ever possible or would she choose to pull herself up and seek the light? The crossroads had been reached, where only she could save herself. No one else could do this for her. Would she sink, or swim?

As I read her words, something resonated within. I felt as though I was drowning, being swallowed up by the darkness and the enormity of what had happened to me. I couldn't breathe properly, my chest was constricted and my body felt so heavy, carrying this enormous dark weight. I too had reached my own crossroads. Was I going to allow myself to sink even lower? Was this going to be my rock bottom? Was I going to accept that my life was now over?

I considered my options at length and something stirred within me for the first time in weeks. Was I going to allow this miscarriage to destroy me and my entire life? Or not?

I'd faced adversity before. And survived. I survived the never-ending first night of my miscarriage. I'd survived the last few traumatic weeks. Could I find a way to dig even deeper within my very being to connect with my inner resilience and strength once more?

Who would I be letting down if I allowed this trauma to destroy me? My husband, my parents, my family and most importantly myself. This was no way to honour Grace. I had to seek out the light through the cracks. I had to find glimmers of hope for my future. I had to use every ounce of strength and courage I could find to claw my way up out of this pit of despair. I had to rebuild myself and my life. I had to. For me and for Grace. Because what was the alternative?

In this moment, I made an important commitment to myself, in that I would commit to doing my very best to move forwards, repair and re-build and live the best life I could live, for the two of us. I knew this option was going to be far from easy, but I would give it my best shot. Because nothing could be worse than the place I had found myself in. If I didn't take this option and make this choice, then I knew I may as well give up and choose not to be in the world anymore. I realised that this was not the ideal option for me; somewhere within I knew I still had a life worth living.

Once I made this life-changing decision, I understood that in order to move forwards I had to surrender some more and allow whatever came up and not try to push it away. I also listened to what I really needed and knew that my body, mind and soul needed to rest for as long as it would take to feel better. It was time to retreat and reflect and take much needed time out from my business, until the end of the year at the very least. And just give myself the permission and space to begin the long journey of grieving and healing.

Everything didn't miraculously change overnight, but slowly with each day that passed I felt a little better, brighter and regained some physical strength. With my only focus now being on tending to myself and my immediate needs, I didn't need to waste precious energy trying to pretend to anyone else that I was OK. When I accepted that this was the only thing I had to do, suddenly instinctively I realised I was being guided. I began to notice a gentle inner voice talking to me that had a deep, profound comforting presence. This voice continued to nudge me forward moment-by-moment and day-by-day, gently whispering to me to keep me going:

> *'Come on get up and get yourself dressed, put on your nice*
> *clothes that make you feel good.*
> *Eat nourishing food that you love.*
> *Let's do the little things you enjoy.*
> *Talk and let yourself cry, release your tears.*
> *Write in your journal.*
> *Grab your pencils and colour-in.*
> *Let's go outside after dark for a walk.*
> *Keep on walking, then do a little more.'*

This voice was comforting. I instantly trusted this beautiful presence. I totally surrendered to the pain and grief. I began to open up to listen and follow the guidance I received. Which meant I felt a little less alone.

Somehow I knew this voice. It sounded familiar. Eventually it dawned on me how I knew this presence. This voice, this beautiful soul right by my side whispering to me, encouraging me forward was our angel Grace Rose.

Our time together wasn't over, she hadn't completely gone or disappeared from my life. I experienced a deep profound inner knowing that despite everything that had happened we were still connected. Mother and daughter were spiritually entwined. Our bond had not been severed when she left my body. Because now I realised she had another purpose, my beautiful angel Grace was gently guiding me, her mother, back towards love, the light and a completely different way of life. Which had to be worth living for the both of us.

CHAPTER 5

ACCEPT YOUR INNER KNOWING
WITH GRACE

Soon it was mid-December; Christmas was looming and I could not face going out during daylight hours. I still didn't feel up to talking to anyone or relish being seen, so decided to venture out after dark just to get myself out of the house and get some gentle exercise. At the top of our road there was a church with a graveyard, leading to a short cut through to the main road. Even walking through the gravestones in the dark no longer frightened me. It seemed nothing did. I realised my biggest fear of becoming pregnant and losing another baby had already happened, so I no longer cared what life chose to throw at me.

Whilst walking, the tears came in abundance. The movement, pace and rhythm of my steps enabled all the emotions to spill out unguarded. This was a cathartic time to be alone with my thoughts and move my body as well as shift my energy. Walking alone after dark became a daily ritual, as I felt my physical strength return my pace quickened, often determined by the amount of anger and anguish I felt in the moment. Often my thoughts would be stuck in a downward loop, going crazy and wanting answers as to why this had happened to us. Did I deserve this to happen? Why do other women have babies so easily – even if they don't want them in the first place? If I got pregnant again would it happen once more? Where had Grace really gone? The questions buzzed and raced through my mind. Why was life so cruel and unfair, hadn't I been through enough? On and on it went, never ceasing.

The one thing I didn't blame was my body. Miraculously it had been the longest pregnancy I had experienced, so this was a little encouraging. I knew I could conceive and I knew an embryo could implant successfully. But I still didn't have a definitive answer as to why I had miscarried. The doctor I'd seen at the EPU couldn't tell me either, but because it was a missed miscarriage it was more than likely to be due to a chromosome abnormality. Something amiss genetically and nature's way of screening and preventing the pregnancy from continuing naturally any further. However difficult this was to accept I began to learn that there are many reasons for miscarriage and sometimes there is no obvious reason. There are also different types of miscarriage. I continued to need answers to big life questions and actively sought meaning from our loss. I didn't want to blame anyone or anything but struggled to comprehend why horrific things happen in life to some and never to others. Why do they even have to happen at all?

As it was so close to Christmas, houses were lit with twinkly lights and festive decorations. Shop fronts were full of gift ideas and delicious seasonal foods. In our town square a magnificent Christmas tree was the magical centre piece. As for me, I felt numb and full to the brim with sadness. Living in my body, but not fully present to the world at large. There was absolutely no festive cheer or joy within me at all, but day-by-day as I walked I noticed and felt drawn to the glimmers of light within the darkness that surrounded me, enticing me forwards.

In the run up to Christmas we received lovely messages and special gifts from kind-hearted friends and family, who told us we were in their thoughts and so was Grace. However, on the flip side we also experienced absence and silence, especially from friends who I once believed I could rely on no matter what. Ultimately I knew I had to rely on and fix myself, no one could heal my broken heart except me. I had reached the crossroads and made the choice to rebuild my life and seek out light and joy again. Hadn't I?

From the bottom of my life and within my darkest moments, the gentle voice would continue to show up to encourage me. It transpired this voice was persistent and wasn't going away, it was getting louder. I wondered if I had gone completely mad. I was not in a fit state of mind to be able to tell either way. But I continued to listen and pay attention. Surely this wasn't doing me any harm.

Throughout my life I've always been intuitive, getting magical hunches or remarkable insights about people or situations, and the older I've become the more I've learnt to listen and trust my intuition and follow the guidance. There are times when I've known and received clear insights about something or someone before it happens in real life. In fact, my sister has always charmingly referred to me as a witch. I've never questioned this gift and these hunches have only proved to serve me well. So why would I begin to doubt them now? I wasn't going mad or delusional, how could I be when I knew within the depths of my soul, that this voice I could hear comes from Grace. It just had to be so.

As we had already named Grace prior to the miscarriage she remained significant, not anonymous. And we found it comforting to refer to her by her name and wanted her to be remembered as Grace Rose. Not only as that baby you lost. It seemed odd to some people around us that we had chosen to name our baby. Looking back, it didn't seem odd to us; Grace enlightened us and let us know precisely who she is. This was to become one of many things I had to navigate around other people's opinions about how we should handle our loss. Whilst connecting with others and reading more stories of miscarriage, I could see that it wasn't only us who decided to name their baby. Many parents-to-be name their babies so that they will be remembered and acknowledged. Others may find this odd and feel uncomfortable to speak your baby's name out loud. But I realised this wasn't about them and began to care less about what anyone else thought of us. This wasn't something up for discussion, justification or scrutiny. However I noticed and appreciated when others followed my lead and called Grace by her name too.

In addition to losing Grace, I'd lost trust in life, in humanity and in some of the people around me. People who I had once whole-heartedly believed and referred to as my friends. I wondered where were the friends who I believed would always be there in any time of trouble or strife? No one willingly wants to be around someone who has hit rock bottom and is in the depths of grief do they? Maybe it is better to give them space and stay well away, until they re-emerge. Maybe it is easier to avoid them than having to witness someone else's pain. But when it's you, and you are the person who is suffering you need your friends to show up, as the very last thing you need is to feel even more alone and isolated than you already do. Navigating a traumatic loss means you start to question everything and everyone. You see life differently. Everything becomes heightened and illuminated. You realise who is there for you no matter what and who unexpectedly turns their backs in your time of need. I began to care less about those who really couldn't care less about us. I had no interest in what others thought of me. But what I did care about was who and what really mattered to me. I began to see people differently and would no longer allow or tolerate flaky friends into my most trusted inner circle. It became transparent who did not have my best interests at heart. All they cared about was their own lives. This was a tough lesson to accept. And it would only get harder as the weeks passed by.

Prioritising my own self-care, well-being and healing was at the top of my to-do list and every day I would try and seek moments of light and joy, however small. Riding the tidal wave of grief became a much-needed life skill, there was nowhere to hide from my feelings or emotions. If I tried to fight them or push them away, they would only fight back harder, so I had to accept that I needed to allow myself to feel everything, and just be OK with whatever decided to come into my awareness.

The other big thing I couldn't escape was Christmas, it was getting closer and I preferred to bypass it completely if I could. Christmas is always a special time of year for us, one we celebrate by getting together with family and loved ones. But the last thing I wanted to do was celebrate anything. How could I, when only a few weeks before I had lost my longed-for baby. In my mind there was absolutely nothing to celebrate. Despite my resistance and the absence of any festive cheer, my husband repeatedly asked what gifts I would like for Christmas. There was only one thing I desperately wanted but I couldn't have her. She'd gone. My mum continued to ask when I was going to write and send my Christmas cards. How could I attempt to send cards wishing others a wonderful, merry time or pretend to be filled with joy when I was completely and utterly filled with never-ending sadness. They both persisted, as did the gentle voice within, encouraging me to go out during the day to get some supplies for our Christmas festivities.

Eventually I braced myself to go out during daylight hours. I got myself ready and left the house. As I approached my car one of my neighbours came outside and called me over to her. Damn it; I knew I'd have to make conversation. I walked over to her and as I got closer she enveloped me in the biggest, warmest hug. This was a beautiful, amazing hug. As she kindly held me tightly, I sobbed in her arms and totally went to pieces. This was not meant to happen. At the time we lived in a tiny road, a bit like Coronation Street, and knew most of our neighbours well. They had celebrated with us when they knew we were expecting only now both of us were crying in the road. She told me how sorry she was and that she had been praying for us both and for little Grace. She said her name. To me; out loud. This acknowledgment, her kind prayers and beautiful hug meant everything. A little piece of humanity was restored. With black streaks of mascara running down my face, I told her that this was my first trip out in daylight for weeks. She told me reassuringly that I would find my way again, just to give it more time. She offered her open door and invited me in anytime I needed to talk or to just be with someone else to feel less alone; her door would always be open at any time. I appreciated her love and kindness as she could have watched me leave my house and stayed safely inside and said nothing. But she didn't. She stepped outside, she reached out and offered herself and her support to me at the time I needed all the loving kindness I could find in the world.

We said our goodbyes and I crossed back over the road to my own house, sorted out my face, applied some more mascara and tried again, making another attempt to integrate back into the real world. My mission was to find and purchase our Christmas supplies and when I returned home it was mission accomplished, my arms were full with a brand new Christmas tree, a packet of cards and some sparkly new decorations. I also found an angel to hang on the tree especially for Grace. She wasn't going to be forgotten, she would be remembered and acknowledged this Christmas. That I could control. I tried my best to get into the spirit of Christmas for my husband and for our families. Especially as my sister-in-law would be visiting us from Australia.

Putting up the Christmas tree and decorating our house

gave me something positive to do. I had become engrossed in the task when there was a knock at the front door. I wasn't expecting any visitors therefore I was in two minds whether to answer. I put down the box of decorations and opened the door. I couldn't believe it; standing on my doorstep was my friend Claire. She was far from local and lived three hours away from us in Dorset. What on earth was she doing on my doorstep? It was an incredible surprise, she had decided to pay me a visit, unannounced as she wanted to see for herself how I really was. Once more I found myself enveloped in the biggest hug in the world. This was becoming a regular thing, kind people seemed to want to hug me. I didn't complain and we couldn't let go of each other for ages. Once again, tears streamed down my face and I was so thrilled to see her. This unexpected visit meant the world to me. She didn't come empty handed either and gave me the most beautiful card and a special gift. For me and for Grace. A rose quartz crystal angel, to help heal my broken heart. What a gift to treasure. Sadly she could not stay for long as she was en route to somewhere else, so reluctantly I let go of her so she could leave. It had been a real tonic seeing her, albeit briefly. After she left the tears continued to fall whilst I put up the Christmas decorations and hung my angel for Grace on our new tree.

My faith in humanity moved up another notch. I had to believe there were still kind, thoughtful friends out there. Friends who would unexpectedly show up to demonstrate just how much we meant to them and that they loved and cared about us after all.

Maybe I wasn't as alone in my grief as I'd previously believed.

CHAPTER 6

HOLD YOURSELF TO THE STANDARD OF GRACE

As the December days continued to slowly pass once again my mood plummeted. I understood that there really isn't an escape from the tidal wave of grief and emotion, allowing everything to 'just be' became a daily coping mechanism. I remembered I had a book that had been a source of guidance for many years, written by Betty Shine; her healing books and intuitive wisdom gave her readers hope and encouragement in their moments of need. 'A Mind Of Your Own' is an incredible book full of wisdom and one to dip in and out of when the need arises. Instinctively I felt drawn to it on the bookshelf, picked it up and opened the page to read more on grief.

Betty says: 'Tears shed by those who are grieving are only blessed relief when you are locked in an anguished embrace of memories of things that were meant to be and words that were never said. There is no set time when you should relinquish the cloak of despair and look to the future. You can only do that when the time is right, and because we are all unique, this time period will be different for everyone. It is the act of grieving that, when burnt out, will bring its own kind of peace. And again, as unique beings, it will be an original experience. At these times we need our nearest and dearest. If you are alone, ask for help, if not from someone close then from one of the many organisations that are full of caring people. Do not go through a grieving period alone'.

In the book it suggests a visualisation and when in need to contact a friend along with the affirmation that if you ask you will receive.

Asking for help had not been on my radar, I had always been quite self-sufficient throughout my life, and when troubles arose I tended to muddle my way through and get on with it. But now it was different; I realised I needed to share more with those close to me about how I really felt and to avoid trying to cope alone. Later that morning one of my closest and oldest friends texted me to see how I was. Rather than text her back, I decided to call her instead. I needed to speak to her, not just text. Even though I called her immediately, my call went to voice mail, so I decided to send her a reply via text and said things were really tough for me at the moment. I believed she would call me back, especially when she saw she had a missed call and my response, in that I was struggling.

The path of truth and vulnerability is incredibly difficult, especially when you don't like asking anyone else for help or support. Being openly vulnerable was out of character for me. Typically I'd be a constant tower of strength to my friends. With this particular friend, over the course of our almost twenty-year friendship I had always been there for her, in more ways than one. I'd been a trusted friend and confidant and when her life was in total turmoil I'd helped her find her way out. I'd encouraged her to find a solution. I'd listened without judgement when she dropped the pretense and admitted she'd had enough and wanted to end it all. I re-wrote her CV and found her a new job to ease her financial woes. Then out of the blue she was diagnosed with cancer, so once again I dropped everything so I could see her and offer my support as soon as possible.

And yet when it came to me, it wasn't reciprocated. In my most desperate time of need she never got around to returning my phone call. She didn't reply to my text for another three weeks and made no attempt to check in or visit me in person even though I only lived half an hour away. When she did finally get in touch, Christmas had come and gone, and all she wanted to know was whether I had a good one and asked me to come and visit her. There was no mention of Grace or what had happened at all.

Already being in a fragile state, I wondered why it had taken her so long to respond. Why should I go to her? And why hadn't she made any effort to come and see me? With each day that passed I felt increasingly angry and incensed. I knew without a shadow of doubt she was avoiding seeing or even talking to me in person. We'd been friends for a long time, for many years, and had shared a lot of life's ups and downs together. At the time I believed I could trust her implicitly. I'd believed that our friendship was one with mutual love and respect, a relationship where we'd always support each other whatever life threw at us. But I was wrong.

Over the years, I deliberately hadn't confided in many of my friends; they didn't all know the true extent of my long quest and journey towards motherhood, but she did. She knew all of it. She knew about my struggles and every setback. Other than our immediate families she was the first friend to know I was pregnant with Grace. In fact, unbeknown to us I was newly pregnant the last time I saw her, except we all had no idea at the time. Claire and I had visited for lunch and I mentioned my prawns tasted off, odd and metallic. We'd laughed about my 'awful' prawns afterwards, when we knew the reason why hers were so delicious. She shared my excitement and joy and called me regularly for pregnancy progress updates and texted me every few days. Until it all went wrong.

The last time I spoke to her was the day I'd birthed Grace at home. I was deeply and understandably distressed. I told her I didn't know what to do. For the first time in our friendship, I really needed her guidance and even though she hadn't lost a baby, she had been battling with cancer for the last couple of years and was now in remission. I asked her how did she cope? How did she get through each day? She couldn't answer me. I knew it wasn't down to her to even attempt to fix anything or take away my pain, but I believed she would understand the uncertainty and turmoil I now faced. What I really needed most of all was for her to just be with me, I didn't expect her to do anything other than be there. But she didn't show up; she left me to it.

I felt completely abandoned; the feelings of isolation exacerbated, and I'd wanted to talk to her, to open up and share how I really felt, but how could I now? I felt so hurt on top of the pain and anguish of losing Grace. Only this wasn't the first time she'd behaved like this towards me, she'd left me to my own devices before, but this time I knew it wouldn't happen again, this was going to be the last time she'd ever let me down. All I knew was that if any of my friends had experienced the trauma and suffering that I had, I'd be there no matter what. I'd reach out and give them as much support as they needed. And if I received a missed call from a friend who had only just lost her much longed for baby, I'd return her call immediately. Not wait and get around to replying via text several weeks later.

In addition to the impact of losing Grace, I could no longer ignore how let down I felt. I am not a needy person bouncing from one life drama to another, but the simple fact is I needed her. Trust and loyalty are two enormous values of mine and in good times or bad I expect my friends to show up and do what they can. Even if this is just to make their presence known; to do whatever they can to demonstrate they care. Despite my heartache and distress I deserved more than this. Friendship is a two-way relationship; about giving and receiving. Surely?

More time passed by as I remained within the depths of grief and heartache. This situation was not helping my emotional well-being either. And soon there was a new addition to my list of emotions; rage. Within the depths of grief, every emotion is heightened. You're on a roller-coaster feeling relatively OK and rational one minute and totally irrational the next. You question everything and everyone. When every ounce of happiness and joy has been sucked out of your very being, you lose trust; in yourself, in life and especially in people around you. She contacted me again a couple of months later via another text message, she'd had a quiet moment at work. In between there was still no phone-call or visit in person. It all felt too little, too late. The longer this went on I became less inclined to even begin to open up and confide in her. I no longer wanted to see or talk to her at all, especially when she had demonstrated she couldn't be relied on at the time I had needed her most. Rather than attempt to articulate the anger and hurt I felt via a text message, another friend who had been right by my side throughout, suggested sending her an email instead so that I could express how I really felt. It was not an easy message to write or send, however I tried not to rant or rave, but to be explicit about how I was and what I'd really needed.

Instead of replying to me – she decided the best course of action was to forward it onto someone else to deal with, a family friend, who in turn took the opportunity to present my email message to my mum via her phone when she met her for a social get-together. She asked her, 'What is this all about from Mel?'. This situation had absolutely nothing to do with her and her interference was far from welcome. It only served to incense me and exacerbate an already difficult situation.

Fortunately my mum knew all about the email message,

as she'd already seen it herself, and knew just how much my so-called friend had let me down. But presenting my email message, a message that was sent to another friend, privately; this betrayal was deemed off the scale. My poor mum sat there and explained how much I had been through and that I continued to struggle and suffer. My mum had to stand by and witness the absolute devastation and distress that I, her own daughter, had been through and was still going through. My mum had lost Grace too, her granddaughter. Whoever concocted this plan and thought this was the ideal way forward was completely out of order. It was a wicked thing to do to me and my mum. My lovely mum had been an endless well of support, accompanying me every step of the way, trying to encourage me back to life, how could either of them think this was the right thing to do?

Later when my mum told me what had happened, I could not believe it. How could both of them betray me like this? How could my friend breach my trust in such an appalling way? And how, despite everything, could she still not find the courage to pick up the phone and talk to me directly, or see me in person.

My rage reached new heights. Despite wanting to have it out with both of them, I didn't, I refrained. But only because my mum asked me to. I kept my mouth shut out of loyalty to my mum as I didn't want to jeopardise another friendship with her friend too. I silenced and suppressed my own voice to keep the peace, but I was angry, livid and had had enough of being treated so badly. This was not friendship.

This situation brought another low on top of everything else I had to contend with. As far as I could see this had to be the end of our friendships, the relationships had to be severed as a result. How could there ever be a place for either of them within my trusted inner circle when there was absolutely no trust between us at all.

This became another important life lesson that

demanded my attention; I had to start putting myself first in every sense. Even if it meant friendships I'd once valued ended as a result. I shouldn't have to plead for a friend to come and see me, or even pick up the phone, let alone try to justify my feelings or grief. Should I? I realised it was time to stand up for myself and after loss you're no longer scared to let go of someone who clearly does not have your best interests at heart. Despite my grief, anger, rage and sadness I started to trust in something far more important, the value of my own self-worth.

And so this is how I experienced first-hand how seemingly insignificant miscarriage is, not only to society at large but also to those within my social circle, because I lost other mutual friends too. She'd had cancer; I'd just lost my baby. There was no comparison between the two. Miscarriage and cancer aren't a like-for-like are they? They don't need to be compared on their impact or severity on our emotional health and well-being. But equally they can both destroy lives.

My understanding and expectation of being a good, trusted friend means someone who is there for you and you are there for them; whatever the circumstances; good, bad and everything in between. In the fallout it transpired it was deemed unreasonable of me to have such high expectations of what constitutes a good friend. I've never felt more isolated and judged. It wasn't only me who lost a baby and friends, my husband did too. One of his friends had become a father for the first time to a baby girl, two weeks before my pregnancy ended with Grace. Subsequently my husband has never heard or seen him again since.

As I became stronger I no longer felt the need to even attempt to defend myself or justify my upset. What would be the point? So, I didn't. I let it be and focused on my recovery. I also turned to Brene Brown and her book 'Rising Strong', as contained within is something she refers to as B.R.A.V.I.N.G which teaches how to cultivate self-trust and deepen our relationships with others. Braving stands for

Boundaries, Reliability, Accountability, Vault, Integrity, Non-Judgement and Generosity. Thanks to Brene's guidance I realised that these friendships were well past their sell-by-date and had been for quite some time. Thanks to my miscarriage the blinkers were removed and this situation had demonstrated who they really were and that they were no longer real, trusted friends of mine. I wasn't the same person I once was either, miscarriage and all the associated trauma changes something profound within you forever. You are not the same person you were before.

My phone call was never returned. There was never a visit in person. I will never see my friend again. Two years after we lost Grace she sadly passed away, the cancer returned and her life ended far too soon. We never reconciled, I could not move past her betrayal and she held me responsible for the end of our friendship. Several days before she died, I learned she had been admitted to a hospice. With limited time left I reached out to her and sent a note with my love, light and peace. From mutual friends I heard my message was well received. After she passed, I had time to reflect; looking back we were both in need of support but for different reasons. It took me losing Grace to see that she was not capable of offering her support to me and only she knew her reason why. During a physic reading, a while after she had passed unexpectedly, I received a message. The physic knew nothing at all about my friend – but the message was clear. Someone who had been close to me wanted to apologise, she'd felt guilty for letting me down. She knew she had, and I'd known it too. This message had to be from her, there was no one else who it could have been. For this I am forever grateful as eventually it brought some much-needed closure.

I realise it is not easy to be around someone who is grieving. We'd rather avoid witnessing anyone else's pain and discomfort. It can trigger uncomfortable thoughts and emotions in us too, that we'd rather not have to face. But the fact is every human being on this planet is going to experience loss and grief at some point; there is no escaping this reality. Now I am working towards forgiveness, I cannot forget what happened, but I can choose to forgive. I could have been one of those people who turned away too, except I am glad I am not. Her approach to life, even until the end, was to put a brave face on everything, pretend to everyone else that all was well and try and convince the world that she was coping even if she wasn't. But I always saw straight through this facade, with me there was nowhere for her to hide. I have a gift for seeing people as they really are; especially it seems in the midst of grief. Now I remember all the good times we had together more frequently. It catches me, often at the strangest moments, that she is sadly no longer here.

Sometimes even the smallest gesture goes a long way; despite some of my friendships coming to an end, new relationships formed. The remarkable thing about loss is that you find and connect with kind, loving and compassionate human beings too. There are brave, courageous souls who will step forward, reach out to you with empathy and love and walk alongside holding the space for you, for as long as it takes for you to grieve and heal. You don't have to play down your feelings, you don't have to pretend you're OK, and you definitely don't have to attempt to justify the depth of your loss. They accept you as you are in the moment. They find a way to offer much-needed support and make it known that they are there waiting, if and when you need them. They get it and they get you. Maybe they have even been there too. These are the people we all want and need in our lives. It's only then we feel less alone.

I will always be eternally grateful to those who reached out to us, who expressed their sorrow for our loss and acknowledged our grief and of course Grace. The beautiful cards, notes and gifts we received will always be treasured. Every hug, prayer and kind word was so welcome. And those who continue to acknowledge Grace along with us with love and kindness, I remember each and every one of them.

I continue to believe that having the ability, strength and courage to bear witness to a bereaved mother's grief without flinching, is admirable. To be able to support and acknowledge and be on standby for your friends and loved-ones in need is always helpful. To make it known you are available no matter what is true friendship, and to never judge or wish away their grief is imperative towards their recovery.

If someone you know has lost their much longed-for baby, show up, even if you have no idea what do or say. Just be with them. Hold them. Let them know just how much you care. Speak of their baby by their name if they have one. This is more than enough. Willingly give them all the love, support and encouragement you can.

But whatever you do, don't turn the other way or force them to have to ask you for it.

CHAPTER 7

IN THE END IT ALL COMES DOWN TO GRACE

During my own childhood Christmas was always magical. Our extended family members would come to stay and I'd be evicted from my bedroom and have to sleep on the airbed in my sister's room until our guests departed. We'd try to sleep the night before the big day but found it difficult to nod off, we'd be far too excited anticipating the arrival of Father Christmas and an abundance of presents. As we got older, one Christmas Eve my sister and I woke up and found we'd had a visitor. Our stockings were full of gifts and instead of going back to sleep like good girls should, we decided to open them all there and then even if we had nothing else to open come morning.

As a family we celebrate many special occasions and always get together in one place to celebrate our birthdays, Easter and Christmas. Our families are, and will always be, incredibly important to us. But the older I've become the more I've realised special occasions are bittersweet, especially when you've recently lost someone precious to you. For the first time ever in my lifetime I was dreading Christmas; I was far from a bundle of joy. If someone had given me a permission slip to avoid it that year I would have willingly taken it. But my husband insisted we were going to see our families, despite my reservations and glaringly obvious sadness.

On Christmas Day we made our way down to my in-laws in Kent. My sister-in-law Janine was visiting with her soon-to-be husband from Melbourne Australia, so of course we wanted to see them. She is an absolute joy to be around, full of life, energy and laughter. Seeing her and spending precious time together was a real tonic. She even made me smile and laugh, which had seemed impossible only days before. On Boxing Day we went to my sister's in Surrey and my niece Boo was four at the time. She was filled with all the joy and excitement her mum and I had experienced as children at Christmas. It wasn't as bad as I'd envisaged, being out of the house and surrounded by our loved ones did us both the world of good. For a brief time we could forget everything that had happened and experience some level of normality. Even if only for a few days.

The severity of grief shifts somehow when you least expect it and remarkably glimmers of light, joy and laughter find their way to creep back into your life through the immense darkness. It may not be much initially, but gradually your mind refocuses its attention elsewhere to give you some much needed respite before the waves of darkness pull you back down once more.

I hadn't expected to feel such continuing sadness and heartfelt longing for Grace. Had I not suffered a miscarriage we would all have been celebrating her imminent arrival as well as Christmas. I felt powerless, out of control of my own life and destiny, and all I wanted to do was reach her and bring her back to me, back to us, to her family where she would always belong. But I couldn't. I agonised over where my baby had gone. This primal maternal instinct would not subside. Part of me was now missing. My own inner light had dimmed and almost diminished completely. My heart was in physical pain and my body was heavily weighed down with the intensity of on-going grief. In my frantic dreams, if I managed to sleep, I'd be searching for her. I tried to describe this hideous feeling of separation to my husband. As a child if I lost my parents whilst out shopping, I panicked. I'd be worried, searching for them and thinking I'd never find them again. Eventually they'd find me and all would be well. We'd find each other. Only Grace and I would not.

If I believed Christmas was going to be tough, New Year proved to be even more so. As every new year rolls round, so do the expectations of it being a good one ahead. But as the new year of 2016 began, I was blindsided once more by the loss, pain and anguish. We were supposed to be awaiting the arrival of our precious baby this year. We would have been extending our own little family. We should have been counting down the months and weeks until her due date. We could have been making space in our home for her nursery and deciding what pram to wheel her around in. But instead of all of this – we were mourning the loss of Grace and this continued to be tough for me to contemplate. I felt ever increasing sadness as with each week that passed, all the milestones Grace could have reached during pregnancy were now gone. Forever.

Despite the abundance of sadness there was something that hadn't disappeared; I continued to hear her gentle voice, and surreal nudges unexpectedly arrived, often at the moment I needed them the most. My parents sent us a beautiful bouquet of flowers shortly after I returned home from hospital and I'd already decided to order the David Austin 'Grace Rose' for our garden as a tribute to her. Remarkably contained within the bouquet from my mum and dad were gorgeous apricot roses, identical to the Grace rose. I ordered our new Grace rose bush and waited for it to be delivered. I sensed Grace was still making her presence known to us. There would be plenty more little nudges, signs and synchronicities to come.

At the beginning of every new year I chose a word; the word must be powerful and resonate with me at a deep level so that it inspires me in life and for my work in the coming year. As I wondered about what my word for the new year could be, it became glaringly obvious that it had to be 'Grace'. Especially when I spotted this quote right in front of me whilst pinning images on my Pinterest virtual pin-boards:

'How you climb up the mountain, is just as important as how you get down the mountain,
And so it is as it is with life,
Which for many of us becomes one big gigantic test followed by one gigantic lesson
In the end it all comes down to one word – Grace
It's how you accept winning and losing
Good luck and bad luck
And the darkness and the light.'

Reading these profound words gave me shivers, in a nice way. These words spoke to me deeply, and powerfully resonated at soul level. Grace had to be my word of the year, there was no doubt about it.

Gradually something was beginning to shift a little more within me, maybe there could be meaning in our loss. Had this happened for a reason? I failed to comprehend why or what that reason could be. I wondered if we will we ever know or understand why some babies survive and so many don't. I continued to believe that there is something far more powerful than we humans can understand that controls the natural order of life on earth. Maybe we're never meant to know the whys and what-fors. Everything happens as it is destined to. However it's difficult to accept this when it affects you and your own life. Seeing this inspirational quote offered me comfort. I wasn't kidding myself that Grace was still somehow around me, despite knowing and accepting she had gone. I could no longer ignore the overwhelming feeling and inner knowing that her angel spirit continued to be connected to my own. For all my desperate searching and longing hadn't been in vain, instead I began to alter my perspective and trust she hadn't really left us, she hadn't gone anywhere. Grace continued to be with me, all the time. And maybe there is a reason for this too.

With age and life experience I believe in an afterlife; I believe that we are not just human beings and then when we die that's it. I believe we are spiritual beings in human bodies living a human experience. I have no idea why, but this is what I have come to believe and accept. I am not even going to attempt to alter anyone else's beliefs, but these are mine. Because there have been too many weird and wonderful things that have occurred to me in my own lifetime that cannot be logically explained, long before I lost Grace. Therefore I knew I was not crazy. I wasn't seeing or hearing things I wanted to see through the glaze, fog and angst of grief. The signs and synchronicities made themselves known over and over again. And not only for me, my husband would experience them separately too. He is definitely not crazy or delusional either.

Something was opening up within and around us, something greater than I could contemplate or explain rationally. So instead of disregarding myself as nuts, I opened up more and every time I'd hear or see something, I'd pay attention to the guidance on offer. I'd tune in and listen intently. The soft whispers continued; they gave me a sense of comfort. I welcomed them into my world. Grace somehow continued to pop into our lives and reminded us of her eternal presence, in the most unexpected places and moments. As if to remind us that: 'I am always here with you, I haven't left you'.

When I shared what was happening with a member of my family, he asked if I thought I could hear and see these signs because it was what I wanted to hear at the time. Maybe. But as I write our story some three years later and my grief has completely shifted, I know without a shadow of doubt she is here. There is a whole hidden world out there behind the veil, one as human beings we may never truly understand and I believe it is arrogant of us to dismiss this. But it's there all the same. So irrespective of what other people think I know she continues to be with me and it is only this knowing and belief that enabled me to continue to get up out of bed every day ever since and try to rebuild my new way of life.

As the new year got into full swing, I needed to get back to work and felt self-conscious re-emerging and going back into the world. There were several friends and family members who knew I was pregnant and now sadly wasn't. I had deliberately stayed off social media for several months, but to get back to any sense of normality I had to address the elephant in the room. My work and business at the time were online and I ran a social media consultancy therefore I couldn't continue to stay silent for too much longer. I felt it was up to me to address our loss in order to acknowledge what had happened and move forwards.

Just before Christmas we both went out after dark to see the Christmas lights at Kew Gardens. There was a beautiful display of different festive lights that weaved in and out of the trees and around the vast grounds. I'd found it comforting wandering around in the darkness. One display caught my attention more than the others. As we walked towards it all you could see were row after row of lights submerged into the ground. At the very centre of this display was a bright flame, that reached upwards towards the night sky, drawing your eyes and attention fully upwards.

At the top of the flame was a phoenix, rising up, up and away. I stopped walking, totally absorbed by what I could see. I had to take a picture of this magical moment. The phoenix was striking, it was a powerful display. One I've never forgotten. This became the image I decided to use online as a tribute to Grace.

I felt ready to share a post on Facebook, contained within was the quote I'd seen on Pinterest and the phoenix image from Kew. I said that we were sad to leave the year behind and with it our baby Grace. Finally, I thanked those who had been in touch and sent kind messages and thoughtful gifts. Then I pressed publish. Never before had I shared anything so intimate and personal online; it could have been liberating but it wasn't. It felt incredibly sad. But I'd found the courage to share what I needed to and now it was time to move on.

At some point in our lives we are all affected by death and lose people around us that we love. Death is inevitable. However in our culture we are still not encouraged to talk about dying. When we grieve we retreat only to re-emerge when the worst is over. When you lose a loved one, family member or friend, it's likely there will be others around you who share your grief. You mourn the person who has passed together. You're not alone. However, with miscarriage you are mourning the loss of your own baby. A baby who has not yet been born into this world. As a pregnant woman you form a special bond with your baby consciously or subconsciously. The people around you do not feel the same connection as intensely as you do. Therefore this journey of grieving for your lost baby is a lonely one.

Pregnancy is sacred. A miracle. It is remarkable that so many pregnancies are viable and new lives come into our world. From the moment of conception a woman's body, mind and spirit alter and transform to accommodate the impending life creation within. And yet we have been conditioned to disregard this sacred time, the first trimester, just in case things don't work out. Miscarriage is overwhelming because so many women are suffering alone and in silence, feeling emotions they didn't expect to feel. The head may try to overrule the rollercoaster range of emotions that arise in the imminent days and weeks afterwards. But the heart says no; sorry, I am utterly heartbroken.

When you suffer a miscarriage, the natural response is to grieve. The grieving process is essential to allow us to feel what we feel. You cannot think your way out of grief. You can try and suppress it, bury and ignore it and hope that it will go away. But it doesn't, until it has the time and space to be processed in its own unique time. The only cure for grief is to allow it to just be as it is. Grief isn't something to get over, you must delve in and find a way to live alongside it.

Eventually you begin to take painful steps so that you can grieve for your lost baby. You grieve for you and your broken heart. You grieve for the life you thought you'd have. You grieve for your life before this happened. Because miscarriage changes everything, especially you.

I distinctly recall telling myself that the feelings and trauma I felt seemed excessive, over the top and that surely there must be something wrong with me to feel the impact of this so hard. In reality, my life, body and soul had imploded. I was shaken to my core. Everything stopped. But the world around me carried on as though nothing had happened. My heart felt battered and broken. I didn't want to do anything because I couldn't focus and my brain was numb. I couldn't face seeing anyone as I was an emotional mess. The tears would come and I felt like they'd never stop. It transpired my spirit died with Grace and my inner light diminished. What was once me had all but gone, I had been wiped out.

I wasn't supposed to feel like this was I? It seemed others didn't, they just got over it and tried again. But it transpires

I was not the exception to the miscarriage grief rule. Other women felt exactly like I did. I wasn't alone in my heartache, grief and anger. I wasn't the only one and I definitely wasn't alone. There were others out there who were suffering just like me. We were in a sad club together. I knew in order for me to grieve fully I had to talk to others and sought out support groups. The only local one I found nearby was run by the church and even though I am of Christian faith, I am not a practicing Christian so this didn't feel like the ideal solution for me at the time. I wasn't offered counselling on the NHS. I desperately wanted to connect with other women who experienced what I had. I needed to know I wasn't the only one suffering. I wanted to know that what I felt was completely normal. It transpires it was, it's called grief.

I believe that if society positively encouraged women to share and talk about the reality of miscarriage it would go a long way to help prevent the severity and depth of grief felt and the impact on emotional and mental well-being afterwards. We'd know what we feel is normal. We'd receive the encouragement to embrace our true feelings and emotions; all of them as they are. We'd have the acknowledgement that we desperately crave that our loss is significant. We would be able to openly discuss and express our loss without restraint or have to justify our suffering to others. We'd gently find our way forward once more, as long as we were offered the support to grieve and heal in our own good time. And we'd know that regardless of what anyone else thinks or feels, it's only how we feel about our baby that really matters.

As the new year really got underway there was a big question I desperately needed an answer to: 'What could I do now, how could I ever come back from this?'. It was time to tune in, listen to the wisdom of inner guidance within and wait patiently for the answers to arrive; oh and begin the next chapter of my life. I felt ready to make a start on healing and rebuilding my shattered broken heart, with Grace.

I was to learn that my experience of seeing the phoenix at Kew Gardens that night was far more significant and meaningful than I had realised at the time. I know now that this is where I let go of my old life forever and began to connect with my inner strength and my own resilience so that I too could rise like a phoenix and be reborn from the ashes.

GRIEF

"I had my own notion of grief.
I thought it was the sad time that followed the death of someone
you love.
And you had to push through it to get to the other side.
But I am learning there is no other side.
There is no pushing through.
There is an absorption.
Adjustment.
Acceptance.
And grief is not something you complete.
But something you endure.
Grief is not a task to finish and you move on from.
But an element of yourself.
An alteration of your being.
A new way of seeing.
A new way of self."

Author - Gwen Flowers

CHAPTER 8

OPEN YOUR BODY, MIND, HEART AND SOUL TO GRACE

It became a struggle to get to sleep at night. If I managed to drop off, suddenly I'd wake up panicking, with the overwhelming feeling that I was suffocating in the darkness. I'd be hot, sweating and gasping for fresh air, desperate to escape, searching for a way out, totally disorientated and filled with doom. It took some time to calm myself before I could settle down and try to go back to sleep. Normally I am a good sleeper, except when in complete darkness and in unfamiliar places. These night terrors repeatedly occurred whilst I was safely tucked up in my own bed at home. The depth of the terror frightened me, as usually I love nothing more than climbing into our cosy bed, snuggling under the covers and falling asleep as soon as my head hits the pillow. But as the evenings drew to a close, I'd feel anxious about trying to go to sleep every night. I felt increasingly exhausted, my body was wrung out and desperately needed the sleep to enable me to recover and heal so I was at a loss to understand what was going on and how I could tackle this.

Then when I thought things couldn't get any worse, the feelings of terror, panic and overwhelm began to show up during the day. It was worse in enclosed spaces, or in busy places with crowds of people. My senses felt overloaded with stress, they were fully switched on, on high alert; warning me danger was all around even if rationally I knew it wasn't. There didn't seem to be an obvious trigger; panic and anxious thoughts would spontaneously arrive and I'd feel the typical stress signs kick in. My body temperature rose, my chest felt constricted, I'd gasp to take a deep breath and there seemed to be little I could do to stop the panic once it had arrived. All I knew was that it would cease eventually, until the next time.

The never-ending cycle of anxiety increased and it was going to take more than positive thinking to overcome, as my mind seemed to subconsciously work overtime to try and keep me from experiencing any more harm and pain. Reluctantly, I went to see my GP and told her what was happening and the frequency of the attacks. My blood was tested and my iron count was found to be too low, therefore I was anaemic and had to take iron supplements immediately. As for the anxiety, I'd experienced quite a traumatic ordeal and was diagnosed with Post Traumatic Stress Disorder, also known as PTSD.

This anxiety disorder is caused by frightening or extremely stressful events. It can happen immediately, or weeks or even months later. Symptoms include sleeping problems, anxiety, being on hyper alert for perceived danger, physical sensations including sweating and trembling and nightmares about the trauma. Well I ticked all of these boxes.

Often the severity of PTSD after baby loss depends on the level of emotional support received immediately after the miscarriage occurs, and I hadn't had any, not even counselling. Therefore, it finally made sense that following my own traumatic event with the loss of Grace, I began to suffer during the night which quickly escalated to full-on anxiety 24/7.

When I returned from the surgery I began to conduct my own research into PTSD. I came across a study for the British Medical Journal by Imperial College London on the emotional effects on women after miscarriage – '*Post-traumatic stress, anxiety and depression following miscarriage or ectopic pregnancy.*' It made fascinating reading. They concluded that if there were emotional well-being checks and follow up appointments for women immediately after their miscarriage and subsequently at regular monthly intervals, this would help manage and reduce the impact of PTSD in the long term. As for those women who did not receive any emotional well-being checks following their traumatic miscarriage, they were likely to experience moderate to severe anxiety, and in some cases full blown PTSD.

Whilst this study did enlighten me on the severe impact of miscarriage, I realised that many women, just like me, had no idea our suffering could be detrimental to our emotional and mental well-being going forward. The report validated what I felt and experienced; that miscarriage is a traumatic event and that the traumatic memory can be retained within our conscious and sub-conscious mind for years to come. Any trauma we experience in our lives can be stored within the body energetically and may over time release itself and heal. But what if you've been conditioned to play down your miscarriage and don't recognise the fact you're grieving? What if you don't feel allowed to be sad that you are no longer pregnant? What if you know you're suffering but cannot express this to others around you or know where to go for support? What happens to you and your emotional well-being then?

There is no doubt trauma is damaging and can have long term consequences on our healing and recovery. If unacknowledged, suppressed and swallowed down, it festers and blocks the flow of life force energy within the body. It takes on a life of its own and if untreated becomes more damaging and limiting. Our bodies and minds may go on to create physical signs and symptoms to try and grab our attention and demonstrate all is not well, and there is an inner knowing that there is something significant we must deal with. If we try and ignore, numb or suppress trauma the clever mind remembers somewhere within. Trauma does not go away by itself and consequently the mind programs our fight-or-flight response to take immediate action and kick-in at a moment's notice, even when it is not required. Thanks to long-term stress and trauma our bodies begin to age, ache and feel heavy as if the world is on our shoulders. We feel exhausted, sad and low, unable to feel any real joy or motivation for life. We are disconnected, from ourselves and the world around us. All this emotional, mental and physical stress is extremely difficult to come back from. But not impossible.

When I received my own diagnosis and read the report, finally I knew everything I felt was completely normal. There was nothing wrong with me as such, my thoughts, feelings and heartache were all perfectly justified for a woman who had recently lost her much-wanted baby. This reaffirmed the fact that I had been through an awful experience that almost killed me physically, emotionally and spiritually. Somehow, I'd managed to get through the worst of it, but I knew there was a long road ahead in my recovery and healing.

Reading this report made me angry, furious even, because I realised that so many women had lost their babies and continue to do so every day, but despite this here we are suffering alone and in silence. As we've been led to believe that miscarriage is just one of those things and so common therefore we should be over them quickly, never mind discussing them openly with anyone else.

I wondered why the impact of miscarriage has been played down in our culture for so long. Why is it women are sent home with the only advice being try again in six weeks. How can we still be kept in the dark and not know the true impact that suffering a miscarriage can have on our emotional well-being? Why are we not entitled or positively encouraged to grieve for our lost babies?

I didn't have any answers, but something stirred within me. I would not be one to put up and shut up. I knew change was long overdue and I owed it to Grace and myself to be willing to talk about my experience with others. Because if I spoke up then maybe others would feel able to openly share their experiences too. Maybe things could be different in the future and no longer taboo. Maybe other women would feel less alone and isolated at a pivotal time where they need all the kindness, support and all the loving care they can get. And maybe all our shared insights could reduce the impact of trauma and severity of PTSD for other women. Because instead of having to fight for acknowledgement of our heartache due to the loss our precious babies, we could instead give all our focus and energy to our own recovery and healing.

My GP offered me medication to help manage the symptoms of PTSD and anxiety, which I declined. I wanted to find my own way forward and would not take any prescribed drugs unless I absolutely had to. I wasn't depressed or ill, I was in the throes of grief for Grace and pills and medication were not going to bring her back to us. There had to be an alternative method to help me.

Initially I started by conducting more of my own online research into recovery after miscarriage. I sought a holistic approach that didn't involve prescription drugs wherever possible and stumbled across a blog post that detailed the impact of grief on our lungs. We tend to use the expression broken hearted following the loss of a loved one, but within our Western culture we are not taught to consider the effects on the lungs following loss. It was a revelation to me to learn that the lungs hold onto and retain grief energetically. In Traditional Chinese Medicine specific emotional experiences can have a physical reaction. Grief weakens the Lung Qi and subsequently physical symptoms arise including pain in your chest. Therefore when grieving you may suddenly suffer with frequent coughs, more serious respiratory disorders and even asthma. Long-term sadness can turn into chronic grief, which hinders the lungs even further. So it makes sense that when you feel unable to let go and fully express your pent-up grief the body begins to experience more and more physical symptoms and on-going illnesses that demand your attention.

With this in mind it was perfect timing when I saw another post online for an eight-week mindfulness course specifically for Mindfulness Based Stress Reduction (MBSR) from the University of Massachusetts. I instinctively knew my next step had to be focused on working towards reducing my anxiety, increasing self-care and healing my lungs by learning how to breathe more deeply and let everything go.

I'd dabbled with mindfulness and meditation before but not quite to this extent. The course was being held online which gave me something relatively easy to do. I didn't have to go out or be anywhere at a certain time, all I had to do was work my way through the course content at home and quietly practice meditating. There were specific meditation recordings to listen to and practice with and our task was to meditate for a minimum of thirty minutes a day. This felt like a long time. I struggled to sit still, especially when I felt I couldn't concentrate fully and my mind was still a jumble. But I knew I had to persevere if I wanted to feel better and not be heading back to the doctor asking for a prescription for anti-depressants. It's worth mentioning that I don't have anything against anyone taking medication, however personally I wanted to explore other alternative avenues to see if they could help me first. If I didn't feel that I could cope alone or recover without them, then of course I would follow doctor's orders and take them as prescribed. But I believe grief is a completely natural human response, therefore I choose to explore more natural remedies wherever I could. I wanted to deal with my feelings, not suppress them or numb myself out even further.

During one of the meditation classes we were guided to do our own body scan, to sit quietly and focus on specific parts of our body. This was so we could learn how to notice and pay attention to where we were holding onto any stress or tension within. It didn't take me long to realise that I felt heavy, my shoulders were weighed down and my chest ached, as if there was rope wrapped around my chest keeping me held tightly together. As for my breathing, it was shallow, I sensed I was afraid of taking in too much air. I couldn't face taking in anymore life force, just enough to sustain me and keep me alive. Then we were taught to take a deeper breath, to allow the air to expand right into our bellies, fill our chests to capacity and to hold and release fully, slowly. I couldn't remember the last time I had taken a breath like this.

Then I experienced an intense feeling and felt the traumatic energy held tightly within my chest, it was stuck, still and definitely not budging. It was just waiting, I wondered for what, maybe braced for even more trauma and pain. As human beings we'd much rather avoid dealing with or feeling pain, of any kind. No one wants to be in pain but meditating enabled me to notice and begin to move through my feelings and gently release them. As we were instructed to take in another deep breath, followed by another, slowly I began reconnecting with myself as my chest began to expand further. I understood just how much I had been holding in. All the pent-up emotion, anxiety and stress had been held within my fragile body waiting to be expelled for a long time. Finally I had faced my loss and acknowledged myself with a little more loving kindness.

As I practiced breathing deeply some more, I felt a shift within. I trusted it was now safe for me to try to release this tension and welcome new energy inwards down into my lungs once more. Suddenly thirty minutes had passed and it was time to come back into the room and open my eyes. This meditation practice had given me some respite from the weeks of intense stress and trauma, the fog lifted.

Meditating became a daily non-negotiable appointment in my diary. Each thirty-minute session got easier the more I practiced. Learning how to be more mindful of my breath and body meant I could connect and check-in with myself frequently. I could physically notice and intuitively sense anywhere I was holding back, and I listened attentively to my inner thoughts. Every meditation gave me the daily gift of a pocket of peace; gentle time so that I could tune out from my heartache for a while, just be still and calm my racing thoughts to a slower pace and allow and accept my emotions and feelings just as they were.

Meditation and mindfulness became a go-to healing tool that very gently guided me to notice, feel and release the deeply held trauma and tension held within my body, mind and spirit. The more I managed to practice meditating for a minimum of thirty minutes, gradually the extreme symptoms of anxiety reduced. My chest began to feel a little less restricted, my breath was no longer shallow and I managed to get some sleep. Meaning I could get more adequate respite and rest as I began sleeping more soundly and deeply than I had done for a long time. I'd taken the first step on the long path towards healing my body, mind, heart and soul.

CHAPTER 9

LEARNING NOT TO ENVY
ANOTHER'S BLESSING IS GRACE

As the year progressed the intensity of my grief began to subside a little, we were heading towards spring and the depth and severity of the dark days and winter months receded. I'd love to say that miraculously I was over the miscarriage, but in truth I wasn't. I'd accepted there wasn't going to be a quick or easy fix on my grieving and healing journey. So, I continued to connect with other women online within forums and groups specifically on baby loss. I desperately sought others' guidance on what happened next for them following their own miscarriages. I specifically wanted to know how they'd found their own way forward and wondered if they ever got over their loss and what helped them recover and heal holistically.

The Tommy's #miscourage campaign continued to be a source of much-needed connection and a daily reminder that I wasn't alone. Every day more blog posts would be added to their website with individual stories of heartbreak and loss. I read every story and scanned the comments to see if there was anything else that could guide me too. This is where social media can be a force for good, in connecting us with the very people who know or have experienced similar life tragedies or traumatic events. Especially when no-one within our social circles off-line has a clue of how to support us following our ordeal. We can ask each other questions openly, receive honest responses and get much-needed support.

It was within a post on Facebook that a recommendation for a book caught my eye, entitled 'Sunshine After the Storm: A Survival Guide for the Grieving Mother' by Alexa H Bigwarfe. I grabbed my tablet and downloaded the e-book immediately. This book has been compiled by thirty other women, all of whom share their own stories of loss and offer valuable guidance on how to find your new normal. Because after you lose a baby, life is far from normal ever again. Not only is it beautifully written for mothers-to-be in mind, there is support for fathers and those family members and friends who want to offer their help, but maybe don't know how. All the stories included involved different types of baby loss, but the sentiment behind every woman's heartache was clear to see.

In addition to my longing for Grace, I'd found myself incensed by the lack of support and understanding around me, it seemed I had to continuously justify the intensity of my grief and loss to others. After all, as it was an early pregnancy, how could I be so upset as my baby wasn't really a baby was it? So being able to connect with other bereaved mothers-to-be re-affirmed it wasn't only me, other women also had to put up with unwelcome advice, flippant remarks and unhelpful comments. Amongst the support received were many things said that I found shocking, insensitive and inconsiderate. Sometimes the people around you find it hard to express the right words or sentiment, as we don't all know the right things to say at the right time, even more so if you've just lost your baby. Therefore there are times where it is best all round to let a hurtful comment pass you by and believe they really didn't intend to hurt you even further. And other times, when you know it was really better left unsaid.

One of my friends messaged me to say that there would be a gift in the loss of my baby. At the time I could not see how this would ever possibly be the case. Another decided to post on my Facebook page for me to; 'Think of the song by D-Ream - That things can only get better and they will'. What? I was totally flabbergasted by this comment as how do things get better when you've recently lost your baby? And every time I hear this song now it makes me want to scream.

Probably the most meaningless platitude of all that many of us hear over and over again is 'It wasn't meant to be'. It? Oh you mean our baby wasn't meant to be. Right of course better luck next time, maybe only then it is meant to be.

Someone else decided it was the ideal opportunity to speak up and say one of the most incomprehensible things to me on the day we found out Grace no longer had a heartbeat. I was still pregnant and carrying her little body within mine when she uttered the words, 'Isn't it time you tried IVF now?'. During our phone call she implied I hadn't tried hard enough and because I was getting older I must resort to IVF, as she really didn't want me to miss out on being a mother. I'll repeat that 'SHE didn't want ME to miss out'. How I didn't totally lose it with her at the time I will never know. Maybe it was because I was utterly heartbroken and my only concern that day was what was about to happen to our little baby, Grace Rose. I couldn't even contemplate being without her let alone trying again for another baby to replace her anytime soon. Why is it that miscarried babies seem to be instantly somehow replaceable by another pregnancy?

With regards to my own fertility, I didn't have my head in the sand and couldn't be bothered to enlighten her that I hadn't suddenly reached the ripe old age of forty and decided to try my luck at becoming pregnant. I'd spent a long time trying to become a mother and as Grace was not my only pregnancy, I knew only too well that my biological clock was ticking loudly. The chances of me conceiving were getting slimmer by the day. I also knew that IVF was not the magical solution for us, we were not naive and had been informed whether I conceived naturally or via IVF the outcome could potentially end up in another miscarriage. It was about the ability for my body to sustain a pregnancy, not conceive. This chat was not helpful especially on the day we'd found out we wouldn't be having this baby, it only served to upset me even further and frankly my fertility was none of her business, it was mine.

On top of not-so-helpful comments and other people's well-meaning guidance you have to find a way to cope being around other pregnant women. Honestly, when you've miscarried your own baby you do not feel joyful celebrating other's pregnancy announcements. Because it is not you. You also cannot go anywhere to escape other people's babies. As soon as you're up to venturing outdoors it seems everyone in the world has a baby, except you and decides to push their pram towards you just as a reminder of what you're missing. Just in case for a brief moment you have forgotten.

So other people's pregnancies become harder to endure, especially when one of your friends is pregnant at the same time you were. As her bump and baby grows ever more visible, you are attempting to come to terms with the fact that your own pregnancy has unexpectedly brutally ended. Life can be cruel can't it?

My friend was a couple of months ahead of me in her pregnancy and her baby would be her second child. The truth being that when I lost Grace she was the last person I wanted to see. It wasn't personal; it was about self-preservation. I didn't feel envious of her or her baby, I simply wanted mine back. I felt this was not the time to put a brave face on our loss or ignore my own grief, especially as I knew precisely how far along I could have been, with every significant milestone right there with me, etched in my brain running in parallel to reality.

She sent me kind and loving text messages, but we were both wise enough to know that my miscarriage would make life tricky for our friendship for a while and mutually kept our distance. A couple of months passed before I felt up to accepting an offer to visit her at home for tea. I knocked at the door and there she stood blooming; I could not avoid seeing her enormous prominent bump. With only a few more weeks left until she gave birth, it was not going to be an easy afternoon ahead for me.

We settled down on the sofa with our cups of tea and caught up on the news and she asked what had happened with Grace. I felt OK until our conversation turned towards her imminent birth and she said: 'I know this probably isn't something you want to hear, but it really isn't a barrel of laughs having children. I miss my old life and feel like I have lost myself being a mother'. As soon as the words left her mouth there was a look of regret that appeared on her face. She knew it was not the right thing to say to a friend who had just lost her own baby.

I sat quietly for a moment repeating what she'd said in my mind. Believe me it was a challenge not to judge her or condemn what she'd said or go absolutely crazy in disbelief. I am under no illusion that motherhood is easy, but really, why would she choose to tell me this now? I replied: 'You're absolutely right this isn't what I want to hear, especially when I'd do anything to have Grace back here with me and there is absolutely nothing I can do about it'.

She had a beautiful daughter and a healthy baby due any day and if she understood the gifts she had been given, regardless of the challenges of parenthood maybe she could contemplate, even for a shocking moment, what life could be like if she didn't have them at all?

Of course being a mother and a parent is probably the hardest job in the world and sadly it's not for everyone. However the pain of losing a child is unlike any other. You are left with a gaping hole in your life, heart and soul that cannot be filled.

I think we both realised I was not the ideal person to have this conversation with, I simply couldn't resonate or sympathise. Her confession did nothing to ease my own loss, especially whilst so raw. I would have taken the rough and the smooth of parenting, all of it willingly if it meant I could have my own baby back with me. So I drank my tea, said my goodbyes and left. I knew this would be yet another friendship that wouldn't survive much longer.

But it wasn't all meaningless advice or interference on offer, there were also nuggets of wisdom and plenty of loving kindness, especially by those who understood first-hand. One of my friends, who had also lost several babies to miscarriage led me towards Kristen Neff, one of the world's leading experts on self-compassion who says, 'Self-compassion is where we give ourselves the same kindness and care that we'd give to a good friend'.

When I'd asked her how she healed herself following the loss of her babies she said she had to learn about self-compassion. At first I hadn't a clue what she was talking about. So I began to do some more research online. I understood then that if I wanted to move forwards and allow myself to heal fully, I had to focus on my own well-being first and foremost and try to tune out other people's views and opinions, however well meaning. It was time for me to learn more about how to become my own best friend and give myself all the loving kindness I could, as I would do for a friend of mine had she experienced the same dreadful loss. By giving away my own power to others and expecting them to validate my feelings and loss it had only served to add to my stress levels. I could see that it wasn't up to anyone else to decide on my behalf if my miscarriage was worthy of acknowledgement or support. It was all up to me; and I was entitled to grieve and heal however I chose.

During my meditation practice I began to learn about

the art of acceptance, thanks to watching talks from Tara Brach PhD, a psychologist, author and teacher of meditation, emotional healing and spiritual awakening. Watching and listening to Tara taught me more about how to allow all my thoughts and feelings to arise, without trying to change or suppress them. Why waste any more of my precious energy fighting things I had absolutely no control over?

My own self-care became more and more of a priority. I gave myself permission to retreat and reconnect more deeply with myself and I decided other people's views and opinions were theirs and not mine. I could take their comments on board or disregard them as I saw fit.

Writing in my journal became another anchor; slowly day-by-day things began to shift a little more. I'd become more hopeful and a flicker within me soon ignited into a burning flame. Through my written words on the pages within my journal, I began to accept our loss and knew it was time for me to find and embrace my own new normal. There was nothing I could do to bring Grace back, but I could do something to ensure her brief time with us was not meaningless or ever forgotten.

I could do my bit to change the perception and taboo of miscarriage.

I could continue to connect with other women who had experienced miscarriage too so that all our collective voices were no longer ignored.

I could commit to writing and publishing our book, using my own words to tell our unique story.

I could choose to speak up and use my voice online and off to attempt to break the silence that surrounds miscarriage, for each and every woman who could not.

I could share my truth for me and for Grace.

After this realisation I made a commitment to myself and promised Grace she will never be forgotten, for the rest of my days as her mother I will always unashamedly and proudly speak of her; to anyone and everyone who will listen. Because our brief time together will always be in my heart and our story will never be shrouded in secrecy, shame or silence regardless of whether anyone else around me thinks this is appropriate or not. It is not about them. It's about us. And this is something I had total control over.

Once I'd acknowledged and accepted this truth, a brand-new sense of direction and heartfelt purpose opened up right before me. I was no longer powerless, therefore I took another positive step forward on my healing path. It was time things changed for the better for all of us. I'd make damn well sure of it.

CHAPTER 10

WHEREVER LIFE PLANTS A SEED, YOU BLOOM WITH GRACE

Before I could throw everything at changing the perception of miscarriage, there was another enormous stressful situation dominating our minds and lives; selling our house and moving to a new one. We'd been trying unsuccessfully for almost two years and for one reason or another our buyer would pull out or houses we wanted to buy were sold to others. On the day we learned that I was officially pregnant with Grace, our offer on the fourth house we wanted to buy was accepted. Finally; after so much uncertainty on the home front it felt that life was on the up again for us.

My husband had spent eleven years commuting in and out of west London and it had taken its toll on his health and well-being and of course our relationship, in the sense that we were unable to spend much quality time together. We knew things had to change and so we decided to move to the outskirts of London, which meant he would spend two hours less a day commuting and I could focus on my business in and around central London. Those around us thought we were mad, as most people tend to move out of the city. But it made total sense for us and we weren't looking for our forever home, just a new home in an ideal location that suited us both better for the time being.

As you can imagine we were both already under considerable stress when we lost Grace. Adding a miscarriage into this stressful mix only intensified the pressure on our shoulders. The Christmas holidays had given us some much-needed respite as we had another buyer, had found a house we wanted to buy, and everything seemed to be ticking along nicely. Until a couple of months later in early spring unbeknown to us our buyers unexpectedly pulled out, just as we were about to make it official and exchange sale contracts. We were the last to know and this jeopardised the fourth house we were trying to buy.

This blow floored me once more and I wondered if life could get any worse. After hearing this disheartening news, I met my husband off the train and sobbed in his arms, too stunned to speak. Why was it that everything and everyone seemed to be against us? We deserved some happiness too, didn't we? I'd shown this particular couple around our house when I could barely stand up; I was in the midst of miscarrying Grace and still trying to sell our house. They were so insistent they wanted to buy it so I agreed that they could come to see it when really I should have been resting in bed. Later it transpired they liked another house too and had been simultaneously appearing to buy both. But at the eleventh hour decided they wanted the other house more. My faith in humanity reached a new low.

I'd been making steady progress with my emotional health and healing, but this setback wiped me out again. I'd had enough of life. I'd had enough of people letting us down. And I'd really had enough of being disappointed and heartbroken. Everything took its toll on my health, well-being and sanity once more. Trying to move is stressful, life is out of your control to some extent and becomes filled with uncertainty, nothing is a given and it seems you are at the mercy of everyone else's decisions. Our lives became full of ifs and buts and when you're trying to recover from a miscarriage you don't need the extreme stress of moving on top of everything else that you're trying to cope with. It was all too much for me.

But we would not be defeated for too long. During this fretful time my husband and I were tested to the core and yet somehow our inner strength and resilience found a way to kick in under the extreme pressure. There was something else that seemed to be lighting our path ahead. We felt and strongly believed that we were being guided by a magical force outside of us. Because every time we were ready to give up and stay put something miraculous would happen. A glimmer of hope would unexpectedly arrive out of nowhere. Fortunately the woman we were trying to buy from gave us grace, in the form of a few more weeks to find yet another buyer for our house. As we were all so invested in the sales process, she didn't want to put her house back on the market unless she had to, so we tried to sell again.

Out of the blue we found our next buyer, someone who had viewed our property weeks before, had seen it back on the market and wanted to buy. He was a first-time buyer, with nothing to sell, wanted to move quickly and offered us more money than we were ever offered before. It was all positive news; we were elated but tried not to get our hopes up. Just in case.

Even though everything seemed to be against us we noticed little miracles that lifted our spirits, especially the magic of finding coins and lucky pennies whilst out and about. My husband's grandfather always taught him that if you see a penny pick it up and you will have good luck. We took this as a sign that 'Granda' Sammy Dixon, as he was known, was watching over us and sending us an important message; not to give up. As our money jar began to fill up rapidly with coins, we understood that if we were meant to move, somehow we would.

Despite my fragile state of mind, we persevered and even when I believed I'd reached my limit my husband would not give in. He did everything in his power to make our move happen for us as we both desperately needed a fresh start elsewhere.

Whilst still in limbo we went for another visit to see the house we wanted to buy. It is in an urban area but situated next to protected land, a special site of scientific interest (SSSI) with a vast common and a fishing pond. We wandered onto the common and my husband walked ahead avoiding the footpath for some reason. As I tried to keep up with him I looked down, just as something shiny caught my eye, and there gleaming in the grass was a perfect silver twenty pence piece. I shouted out to my husband to come back and see the treasure I found. I held out my hand so he could see the coin and we both smiled and laughed as he said: 'how on earth have you found that here?' It was incredible to find this coin in the grass, and we took this as another sign that we had found our new home, we just had to be a little more patient and hold our nerve.

As the weeks passed our move date was delayed, there were more setbacks and even more stress. Our belongings were packed into boxes despite us not knowing for certain if our move would actually go ahead. Against all the odds stacked against us we finally moved in May, one month before my due date with Grace. Our car was packed to the brim with boxes, our beloved cats Billy and Lola meowed in their baskets and we had even more precious cargo on board, the money jar. Miraculously filled with over twenty-five pounds we'd collected in coins whilst attempting to move. As we said goodbye to the house and town we'd lived in for eleven years we drove up the M3 motorway towards London. I knew this was the end of a significant chapter in my life, it was time to let go of the past, start over and create our brand-new life together.

Instead of the homely welcome we'd envisaged, when we arrived at our new house we were greeted with overgrown gardens and a property buried under a jungle of out-of-control wisteria. The previous owner had moved out several weeks before leaving the inside filthy. Despite all the mess and chaos, instantly I felt a welcoming energy from the house, as if it knew we would lovingly take care of it and restore it back to its former glory. It had taken every ounce of inner strength and resilience to get us here and it was difficult to know where to begin. Fortunately, my parents helped us move and my dad began to work on tidying up the front garden. My mum and I cleaned inside so that we could begin to unpack our belongings and my husband did odd jobs inside and out. The garden S.O.S team arrived the following weekend in the form of my extended family and in return for being fed and watered, we all tackled the back garden together. With the grass up to our knees and weeds and ivy taking over every available space, at the time it all seemed insurmountable. A week after we moved in my husband had to return to work and everything looked and felt so much better; we were exhausted but happy to finally be in our new home.

The house and garden became my new project and I'd spend every available moment I could outside; the hours would whizz by in a blur. I gave what little energy I had left to our new home and garden and miraculously as I did so it began to work its healing magic on me. After so many months of excessive stress, anxiety and trauma I desperately needed the respite from everything; moving, friendships and the miscarriage. Our new surroundings quickly became a sanctuary, providing me with much-needed quiet tranquil space where I could begin to process everything that had happened over the last few years.

I love gardening and being outside, however our new garden was huge, three times bigger than what we'd owned before. It was hard manual work digging out flower beds, cutting back the overgrown ivy and brambles and creating the space for new plants. Eventually I could see the garden had once been carefully tended but had grown wild since the previous owner's husband passed away several years before. As the garden slowly came back to life as a result of hard work and tender loving care, I knew being immersed in nature was also enabling me to heal and recover at the same time.

Scattered around the garden were gorgeous rose bushes. Roses are special to our family and my love of roses descends from my dad. As a family we have always given each other rose plants as gifts in celebration, for anniversaries and in remembrance of loved ones. Our family home has beautiful roses everywhere, climbing up the front of the house, in the beds and within many pots in the garden. So when we left our old house, I couldn't leave my own roses behind, they were all dug up and moved with us too.

In our new garden, my mum dug out the flower bed alongside the garage and within the debris we found an old bench. The seat was rotten but the iron ends could be restored, so my dad took it away to be repaired. 'Grandad's Bench' has a special spot now overlooking the pond and the common. Before we bought the house we knew there was a hidden path down to the pond from our garden, but had no idea how beautiful and tranquil this spot could be. The steps behind our gate had been buried under soil for years and as everything was cleared my husband noticed something sticking up out of the mud under another bush and discovered a stone angel cherub with little wings. The previous owners never had their own children and this cherub once belonged to them. I immediately knew we'd found this cherub for a reason and I cried when I saw her.

I sensed the cleaned-up flower bed alongside the garage was the ideal spot to begin planting and decided this was going to be home for our very special Grace Rose. She had been sitting patiently in a pot on the patio and as my due date approached I knew it was time to create a place of remembrance in the garden especially for her. 'Grace' is a David Austen rose with beautiful apricot petals which are darker in the middle and lighter around the edge; it is stunning. But Grace wouldn't be alone here, alongside I planted our wedding rose bush with deep red roses. Next in line came 'Rhapsody Blue' my dad's rose, a vibrant yellow bush for my mum, then a beautiful pale pink precious rose 'Emily' which my dad bought each of us when my niece Boo was born and finally a softer yellow rose for my sister. Beautiful roses planted all together in one spot in the garden with Grace. And of course, not forgetting the angel cherub and a metal dragonfly we'd also found, placed in the bed too. On the other side of the garden I planted another treasured rose bush 'Amazing Grace' which had been given to us as gift from my friend Claire, with stunning vibrant pink roses, she sits next to 'My Lovely Dad', 'My Lovely Mum' and in memory of Granda Sammy 'Grandpa Dickson'.

One day as I was sitting in the garden admiring all the roses which were in bloom an exquisite blue butterfly sat on my shoulder and flew onto the petals of the Grace Rose. 'Hello sweetheart' I said, my heart filled with joy, knowing Grace loved her new home just as much as we did.

Nature is a remarkable healer and continues to work its magic. Within the sacred sanctuary of our garden mother earth began to gently take care of me. During the spring and summer I began to feel more peaceful, grounded and noticed the abundance of wildlife all around us for the first time. I heard the birdsong and loved seeing the butterflies, dragonflies and birds fly around me. The glimmers of natural beauty touched my heart and soul and provided much needed comfort. Even in solitude I began to feel less alone than I had done in a long time. Nurturing and mothering my plants gave me a renewed sense of purpose and wonder again.

Gradually we got to know our new neighbours too, the gentle cows and cheeky horses that roam freely on the common. The beautiful birds that flutter around us and nest in our trees, the ducks that quack and come into the garden when they want to be fed and not forgetting the noisy diva geese who wake us up in the mornings. Occasionally the heron will pay us a visit and dives in and out of the water catching fish. Frogs jump across the garden; squirrels jump and chase each other between the trees and foxes have made a den on the bank. And then there is the graceful swan, who kept me company and sat quietly in the water below and watched over me as I worked in the garden.

Gardening became my go-to therapy and I'd head outside regardless of the weather. Being outdoors immersed in nature and noticing the seasons and the elements brought me back to a different way of living and being. We believe we were led here; we ended up living precisely where we needed to be. This special place needed us as much as we needed it. After all the years of disappointment and setbacks our patience was eventually rewarded, every day we are filled with gratitude and love for our special home and of course for the magical garden and all the wildlife that surrounds us, for taking us firmly under their wings.

When we moved in, we had no idea just how beautiful the views would be from the garden and the back of our house. Now we've managed to bring more of the outside in, from every window at the back of the house you can see something spectacular. There is beauty in abundance with striking sunsets that take my breath away and the wildlife that's become our tribe. We notice everything going on around us like never before. Being connected to the seasons and cycles of life, meant nature nurtured me back towards the light and a very different way of being.

This remarkable place has become our home and special sanctuary, it also has a name 'Rosewood House' for all the beautiful roses that surround us, and of course in loving memory of our angel Grace Rose. She moved in here with us too and now has her own special place in the garden where we can always remember her.

The positive benefits of nature and gardening on our mental health are now being recognised, as I learned more about nature, the changing seasons and cycles of life and death it helped me focus on being in the moment and to try to stop worrying about the past or my future. Just like my plants and roses, I had to trust in the power of nature and believe the time would come for me to re-emerge and bloom once again.

CHAPTER 11

I KNOW THAT I LOVE YOU MISS GRACE

The following spring, at the age of forty-one I had to face up to the fact that as well as grieving for Grace, I was also now grieving for my dream of being a mother. I couldn't escape the reality that time and my age were no longer on my side and both were a significant factor in whether I'd ever become pregnant and give birth to my own child. I wondered if my life was worth living without my own children. That if I never had my own baby who would I be? How could I ever fill this gaping void in my life?

This led to soul-searching and questioning everything in and around me including my purpose in life, my marriage, my work and relationships. I had to consider what I believed in. What did I value? Who was I as a person and a woman? And what did I want for the rest of my life if my own children were no longer a part of it? There wasn't a plan B; I never thought I'd be in this situation in my forties with no children to speak of. This wasn't how my life was supposed to play out.

Homeopathy has been a constant go-to holistic remedy throughout adulthood and during a consultation with my trusted homeopath Elizabeth Courtis, we discussed the next steps to support my healing path. I'd realised it was time for me to let go of living month-to-month waiting for a miracle and I desperately needed to take back some element of control over my life and destiny. I'd spent so long patiently waiting to become pregnant and have a baby that I hadn't considered any other alternative. Could there even be one?

As well as being a brilliant homeopath, Elizabeth is full of intuitive wisdom and knows me well. She has been treating me with homeopathy for twenty-five years and knows all about my past and present. As we talked she encouraged me to alter my mindset and perspective to see if I could find another way to begin to believe in myself and irrespective of becoming a mother, to know that I am still enough in my own right as a woman. She emphasised that my life could be meaningful with or without children. She guided me to consider all the good around me instead of solely focusing my attention on what I felt was missing.

In addition to self-compassion it transpired I needed to learn more about self-acceptance. I needed to accept myself and my life for what it is, instead of always wanting it to be different. I realised my life could be purposeful and full of meaning, but only if I made the conscious choice for it to be so. I also needed to acknowledge that I did have a good life, and my life was still definitely worth fighting for and living to the full. For me and for Grace.

My husband and I had always had a supportive, loving relationship. But I'd felt we could never be enough without our own children; something was always missing. This perspective began to shift as I realised that we were fortunate in so many other ways. For some couples losing their baby can shatter their relationship, but for us losing Grace brought us even closer together. I am a proud wife; my husband and I have been together for nineteen years and I love him and still like him as a person. These days it can be easy to give up on a marriage during tough times, but I know that our time together is precious and there is no one else I'd rather spend my life with. As I began to reflect and noticed and appreciated all the many good things in my life, I wondered if maybe there could be a Plan B after all.

The challenges and traumas we face throughout our lives can go on to shape us, transform us into new wiser beings, shift and alter our perspective, change our once firmly held beliefs and views and create a new normal. Gradually I could see, and began to believe, that it is possible to find a greater meaning and a new sense of purpose after devastating loss. So I took another important step forward on the steep uphill climb to meet my own new normal and renewed sense of purpose.

Connecting more deeply with myself was the beginning of important and powerful inner-soul work, which would enable me to continue to grieve and heal properly. There is no quick or easy fix to heartache and this necessary work couldn't be rushed. For the first time in my adult life I asked myself the question; 'what was it I wanted and needed now?'. It was time to be honest with myself and the answer arrived almost immediately. I craved time-out; I wasn't anywhere near ready to contemplate trying yet again for another baby, regardless of feeling the pressure of my age and biological clock. My overriding fear was becoming pregnant and losing yet another baby, even the thought of this potential outcome felt far too much to cope with. I knew it was the right time to take a pause on the baby front, give myself a break and start living life again. As I reached this decision a heavy weight lifted off my shoulders.

When you hope to become pregnant you tend to avoid over-committing to anything in the future, such as holidays, long-haul travel or even work projects, just in case your circumstances change. Just before my birthday in March, my sister-in-law Janine announced her engagement and informed us that their wedding would be taking place in Bali the following new year. We held off making any travel arrangements for several months as I'd said to my husband that if I were to become pregnant again I would not risk travelling so far. But with the conscious decision to stop trying we committed to going to Bali and therefore had something positive to look forward to. As well as being at the wedding, we'd also have the opportunity to spend quality time with my husband's family, including our gorgeous nieces and nephews who live in Australia and Spain.

Another great thing in my life is I am an auntie. I love being 'Auntie Mel' and have a special bond with my sister's daughter Boo. From the minute I knew my sister was pregnant I couldn't wait for her to arrive. It seemed she couldn't wait to meet us either, as Baby Boo was born prematurely at thirty-one weeks and is a force of nature. She had to be to survive. Being an auntie means I get to do the fun stuff such as going on the rides at Peppa Pig World and Legoland, having my hair and nails done in all sorts of glittery colours, dressing up and now Boo is older she calls me herself to let me know her news or to put on shows for me to watch online. I couldn't love her any more than I do, even if she was my own daughter.

All our nieces and nephews hold a special place in our life and hearts. But what continues to be difficult is seeing them grow and thrive and wishing our angel Grace was here with them too. She is missing and I don't ever want Grace to be a secret and hope they will always talk of their angel cousin Grace, even when I am long gone.

Regardless of being an Auntie it doesn't stop the relentless question as to why I don't have my own children. Over the years this question has had me shrinking in shame. I'd waffle on and feel obliged to give a detailed explanation, even to strangers. But I made a decision; I wasn't prepared to play things down or skirt around the subject anymore; I would tell the truth. Our truth. When someone is prepared to ask me why I am not a mother or why we don't have our own children, now they must be prepared for my response.

Now I say we want to become parents but don't know
if it will ever happen for us.
Now I say I was pregnant and had a devastating
miscarriage.
Now I tell them about Grace.

The responses are varied, some nod and acknowledge our loss, others look extremely uncomfortable and wish they'd never asked or quickly change the subject. One person said absolutely nothing and walked away without uttering another word. Yes, talking about miscarriage makes others feel extremely uncomfortable.

Despite this awkwardness I continued to feel passionately about changing other people's perceptions around miscarriage and knew that I owed it to myself and to Grace to speak up. The seeds sown in that part of my life-purpose going forward would be to change the perception and taboo of miscarriage, starting with sharing our own story and the truth of being childless through circumstance. There are many women, like me, who are childless but not through a conscious choice. There are many reasons why a woman is not able to give birth to her own child. Irrespective of our childless circumstances we are treated as though we're less than a woman, that our lives are incomplete and that we are not enough without children. This message continues to play out within our social circles, in society and is perpetuated by the media. The problem is we believed them; until now.

My generation were taught that we could have it all; as women there were an abundance of choices on offer to us. We had the freedom to choose a career, a family or even both if we really wanted. But in reality this has come at a price. Because the tricky thing is that babies don't come to order; neither do relationships. Life does not always go to plan. You may not find a partner to have children with, you may not be financially able to have a child, and you may not physically be up to it the older you get. Therefore maybe we don't all get our happy ending. Having a healthy pregnancy and bouncing baby is not a given. Yet within our culture and social conditioning this is taken for granted; that if you choose to have a baby, you'll have one. Sadly, I am still in the camp that hasn't. Yet. So maybe in reality we can't have it all, after all.

Many women and couples struggle to conceive for all sorts of reasons. Regardless of how easy IVF is perceived to be, it is not a fallback solution or even always a success. I haven't experienced IVF, however I do have close friends who have; some had beautiful babies and some sadly didn't. As well as being expensive, if you have to fund every round yourself when it's not offered free on the NHS, IVF is gruelling and there is absolutely no guarantee it will be successful and will have a happy outcome. So many people are struggling with infertility and it is only by talking to each other and sharing our stories about our fertility, pregnancies and miscarriages that anything can ever change. However uncomfortable it is to discuss.

During the summer months life began to settle down to a less frantic and stressful pace, it had been eighteen months since we lost Grace and I felt ready to venture out into the world again and went back to work running my online consultancy business. At the time I worked with women who chose to work for themselves and run their own small businesses. I met up with a previous client and during our session together our conversation shifted to the traumatic events we had both been dealing with since we last met. Sadly, my client had lost her mother and several of her close friends and I had lost Grace. I hadn't spoken openly in a work capacity about my miscarriage and unless anyone asked it was business as usual. But this client knew I had had some time off and asked why. I decided to be honest and told her all about Grace. She listened and was kind and empathetic and went on to open up herself about how she had lost thirteen babies to miscarriage, some several weeks into her pregnancy and another at five months. I couldn't believe how she had endured so much. Eventually she gave birth to her daughter, now a thriving teenager. By us talking openly, we connected deeply and during our conversation she gave me a glimmer of hope, that maybe it wasn't too late for me after all.

As a medium she asked if I sensed Grace's presence and I told her that I did all the time. I explained that I knew she was no longer physically with me, and yet I somehow continued to feel her and experience random signs of Grace unexpectedly. She assured me that my intuition wasn't wrong, Grace is with me and hasn't gone anywhere. In her mind's eye she described her and told me how beautiful she is and that she had dark curly hair. This made me smile and fill up with tears as my husband has very curly dark hair.

I felt the only way I could go on living and cope with everything was to believe that no-matter-what Grace will always be with me, in my heart and in spirit. This enabled me to get out of bed every day, face the world once more and attempt to live my life for us both.

There were too many strange things that continued to happen that couldn't simply be put down to coincidence. After my client meeting, I headed home and drove onto the M25 motorway when a song came on the car radio that I'd never heard before. I had shivers when I listened to the words, 'Oh oh oh Miss Grace, satin and perfume and lace, the minute I saw your face, I knew that I loved you'. I smiled to myself, yet again my angel Grace was with me, giving me a welcome sign and letting me know I was not delusional.

Later I emailed my client to thank her for her insights and told her about the song playing on the car radio. She emailed me back, 'Oh, yes, Miss Grace I know it well. Know it well. Oh, oh Miss Grace, satin and perfume and lace. The minute that I saw your face I knew that I loved you. It was by a 70's group called The Tymes. Whenever you receive an experience of synchronicity, it's Grace telling you she's here, knows how much you love her, and she is loving you. Spirit works with the visual, and sound - all kinds of events coming into our lives are messages. Spirits don't use our low vibratory methods of communication of words, although they will guide us to books, poems, songs on radio and people who will act as a phone mast to speak to us'.

Before we lost Grace, I had been curious to learn more about living a more spiritual way of life. My curiosity escalated as I continued to read other women's stories of their own loss. Many of them believed that even though their babies were not born into this world, they continued to have a deep, spiritual connection with them. This special bond is never broken. Their spirits are infinite and when people ask whether they have children, they say they are mothers to angel babies. So it wasn't only me who felt certain there was something far more deep and meaningful than we can comprehend logically. Along with these insights came another whisper, encouraging me to read a book entitled 'Spirit Babies – How to communicate with the child you were meant to have' by Walter Makichen. This book opened my eyes and intuitive senses even further.

All the signs and synchronicities I'd experienced brought me some comfort and peace. It didn't matter if anyone else believed me or not. I decided I had to do what I felt was right for me and realised another wonderful and important thing, that as well as being a wife and an auntie I am a mother; Grace's mother. I always will be. And she will always be my beloved angel daughter.

Armed with this inner knowing meant life moved forwards more positively once more as I moved closer and closer to my graceful spiritual awakening.

CHAPTER 12

THE EXERCISE OF LOVE AND KINDNESS TO BENEFIT OTHERS IS GRACE

As the seasons changed and we edged into summer the raw grief and emotion began to subside, it became a little easier to talk about the miscarriage and our experience without me continually bursting into tears. I say easier, but it definitely wasn't easy. My husband and I are private people, we're not the type to openly share intimate details of our private lives online or on social media, but we had both chosen to do something to remember Grace therefore we had to be brave and find the courage to speak about our loss publicly.

My husband is sporty and runs and rides his bike long distances, so he and my brother-in-law Wayne (incidentally who doesn't!) committed to taking on 'Ride London' to raise funds for the charity Tommy's. This grueling 100-mile bike ride starts in East London, heads out to the Surrey Hills and comes back into central London, finishing up on the Mall outside Buckingham Palace. 'Ride London' is not an easy challenge to complete even for the most robust cyclist, therefore training began in earnest on a bitterly cold January day seven months before the event.

To coincide with the sponsor page, I felt ready to write and share our story and submitted it for publication online as part of the Tommy's #miscourage blog campaign. As soon as it was published the overwhelming feeling of vulnerability kicked in. I felt deeply exposed. I hated the thought of being perceived as a victim, or as someone to be pitied or even labelled forever as a woman who'd lost her baby, especially on the internet. But I had to accept that this is sadly, now part of my life story.

When trying to raise awareness of anything you want to support, the ideal way these days is to share it on social media, so several of my friends and online connections shared the post with their own social communities. It felt like a runaway train once the post was live; the blog link seemed to take on a life and purpose of its own as it bounced around the internet here, there and everywhere. Once published there was absolutely no going back.

Sometimes it is a careful balancing act to reconcile between the need for privacy and the urge to do something positive, so despite wanting to hide I tried to keep my thoughts upbeat and trusted that if sharing our story helped one other person in need, it would be worth the sacrifice of my privacy. However I realised from this point forward there would no longer be anonymity, especially within my professional life.

Several days after our story was published online I received a welcome message from a friend. One of her close friends had been in touch with her to say that she had read my post and had also suffered a miscarriage but had never felt able to speak to anyone about it. On reading our story she wanted me to know, that thanks to my bravery and courage, she had decided to speak out now too. Receiving this kind message filled my heart with gratitude, as sharing online means you cannot instantly read other people's reactions, unless they decide to comment of course, so you have no idea how your story is perceived. This experience also re-enforced something I firmly believe in, that when you find the courage to share your story and speak the truth with others openly and transparently, it gives them permission and the encouragement to do the same. And so the uncomfortable feeling of over-exposure and vulnerability eased a little more.

It wasn't only me who had to share our story publicly, my husband did too and it wasn't any easier for him either. Participating in a charity event doesn't mean just showing up on the day and hoping for the best, in addition to the intense training programme there are strict fund-raising guidelines to secure your place, you are set a target of four hundred pounds to reach and are encouraged to exceed this if you can. So once again our story and his sponsor page bounced around the internet via email requests and social media posts. We wanted to raise as much money as possible, but we decided to be selective as to where we posted and who we asked for support. Neither of us welcomed any more awkward conversations and we both felt that if we'd been trying to raise money for a cancer charity or something similar it would have felt a little easier to circulate. Admitting we'd lost our baby evoked such a mixed response, that even with our determined fund-raising efforts the stigma around miscarriage and navigating other people's judgement always seemed to be at forefront of our minds. They'd feel uncomfortable and prefer we hadn't mentioned anything.

Our expectations were high; we believed we could smash the target set and that all our friends and families would support us for this amazing cause. As donations came in it was incredible to see the amount raised rise and to receive wonderful encouraging messages of support. It was remarkable how generous people were, especially those who didn't know us well, if at all. But still they donated their pounds and pennies. As people read our story others within our social circle began to share their stories. We were no longer the only ones who'd lost babies, others had too.

Gradually by speaking out and sharing we were making a little difference.

On the flip side of this was the silence. Deafening silence from family members and so-called friends in our social circles who chose to say absolutely nothing. Our donation requests were ignored and whereas we understood that money can be tight and not everyone can donate, we found it hard when they said nothing either. There were no messages of support or encouragement for the boys. Nothing at all. And yet, the clever thing about social media is that it can tell you who sees your posts online, so we knew our messages had been seen. But nevertheless ignored.

I felt extremely hurt and disappointed that people we knew very well couldn't support at all during our time of need or even when we tried to do something positive. We'd never ignored their children; we'd always contributed to gifts and sent cards and messages for birthdays and celebrations. And yet when it came to us and the memory of our own baby Grace, they chose to ignore it all and I've never forgotten that.

Tommy's is an incredible charity that supported us through the darkest days of our lives and yet when those around you cannot utter a word of support, you begin to see them in a very different light. As you're rebuilding your life you notice everything in more detail therefore some relationships and friendships change or end entirely. Suffering such extreme trauma and loss makes you re-evaluate who you surround yourself with and you no longer have the capacity or tolerance for fair-weather friends or even family.

Disappointment aside we remained focused on our intentions, their silence could not derail us, so we intended to honour Grace, raise awareness of Tommy's and the fantastic work they do, raise as much money as possible and of course get both boys round the circuit safe and sound and across the finish line on their bikes.

As the sun rose on Sunday 31st July 2016, in East London twenty-four thousand cyclists crossed the start line for 'Ride London'. Many participated for a chosen charity in memory of their cherished loved ones. Four hundred of the overall riders cycled on behalf of Tommy's and in remembrance of their own babies. This included two very special riders, my beloved husband Darrin and my lovely brother-in-law Wayne, both determined and proud to cycle one hundred miles in one day for our Grace Rose.

I anxiously waited at the finish line along with my in-laws and there was an incredible party-like atmosphere. There was quite a crowd, several people deep, trying to get a glimpse of their loved ones. We were surrounded by supportive families and friends cheering on all the riders by clapping and offering words or shouts of encouragement as they reached the finish line. Every rider was truly magnificent and inspirational, as peddling hard on a bike for one hundred miles takes plenty of resilience and endurance and a lot of training beforehand.

Eventually we spotted the boys riding towards us and Buckingham Palace, and they crossed the finish line exhausted, emotional and jubilant. Both smiling and thankfully in one piece; what a ride and what an achievement. I felt enormous pride for Darrin and Wayne, they'd achieved this together and raised the magnificent amount of one thousand two hundred pounds. Naturally there were tears of joy, and for me also immense sadness, as when the ride took place, had Grace been born she would have been two months old. Despite my heartache, I felt she was elated too and there in spirit, whizzing round the circuit accompanying her daddy and uncle Wayne and cheering them on with us. It was a very special day; one we'll all never forget. The boys loved it so much they went on to do it all over again the following year and raised even more funds for Tommy's.

Being surrounded by people willing to take on extreme

challenges had an uplifting effect; I could see and be reminded of the fact that there are still many good people in the world. Remarkable humans who despite their own traumas and tragedies somehow connect with an inner resilience and find a way to do something positive, all in aid of a good cause. Whether it is taking on an endurance challenge like a marathon or a long bike ride to raise funds and awareness, or even writing and sharing personal stories within blogs, books or articles, these inspirational people find their own way to support others. And whilst doing so are rewarded by connecting with a far deeper sense of purpose and more meaning in their own lives than they ever believed possible.

Finding something positive to focus on goes a long way to aid the healing process, of course it can never diminish your own suffering, but it somehow works its magic and changes you into a better person in the process. As I moved through my own feelings of vulnerability I felt something stronger emerge within me and in my own life. I've since come to learn there is a definition for this shift as I gradually experienced it for myself, it is called p*ost traumatic growth.* As you heal and recover you may begin to have a greater appreciation of life and your own mortality. You realise life can be over in an instant, so you stop wasting precious time or energy focusing on people, places or things that no longer matter. As a result of these changes your relationships with others may improve or diminish completely. You're not the same as before. Realising it isn't forever, you choose to change your entire life for the better and stop putting off things that you'd really love to do. As you do so you learn how to connect deeply with your inner self and find a sense of resilience and personal strength you never believed you were capable of before. And finally, you experience an awakening, encountering profound spiritual change within the depths of your soul, that alters how you view yourself and the world around you. Psychologists evaluate growth in all of these areas following trauma in order to recognise post traumatic growth, and as I understood more I realised I now ticked all of these boxes. Even though at times it felt as though I wasn't making any progress at all, as each month passed I could see I was gradually moving upwards; I was climbing out of the pit of despair. Julia Samuel, a grief psychotherapist writes more about human resilience and how to learn and live following great loss in her book 'Grief Works – stories of life, death and surviving'.

After the ride there seemed to be an extraordinary cultural shift, people started opening up more than ever before and publicly shared their own stories of loss and bereavement online, in the media and on TV. One by one, brave souls talked to others about once out-of-bound subjects that had needed to be discussed openly for such a long time, including depression, anxiety, mental health issues, suicide and baby loss.

Finally the impact of miscarriage hit the news headlines too. 'Baby Loss Awareness Week' is a campaign held every October for bereaved parents across the world to commemorate their babies and to help break the silence and raise awareness of every type of baby loss, during pregnancy and at birth. On the last evening of 'Baby Loss Awareness Week' is the 'Wave of Light', a global commemoration for all babies lost too soon to be remembered collectively. In October 2016 a year since we'd received the happy news that I was pregnant, we found ourselves joining in with all the other bereaved parents across the globe for the first time. A year before we'd never have ever considered this is where we could be. Candles were lit at 7pm local time and images and messages of remembrance were openly shared across social media. As we participated, we could see we were no longer alone in our loss. We lit our own candle for Grace, she was remembered along with all the other lost souls. Her light will never be diminished and continues to burn brightly within my heart every single day.

As long as the open and transparent conversations continue, much-needed change will come. I managed to connect with my own courage and as a result found a new sense of purpose and I am willing to be actively involved in creating this shift and am diligently committed to my cause. These days I often find myself courageously tackling the stigma and taboo of miscarriage in ways I could never have envisaged. I speak at events, I sit on forums to discuss the impact of miscarriage and I blog and share my own insights on my social media platforms. Now having moved through the initial feelings of vulnerability I say 'yes' to sharing our story openly and publicly if it means it might make a difference to someone else suffering elsewhere. And if I waiver and wobble I remember the promise I made to Grace Rose; she will never be forgotten and she is definitely not taboo. This serves to spur me on further.

We continue to support team Tommy's however we can, as this charity will always be close to our hearts. As well as sharing our story for their #miscourage campaign I offered my insights and input to support a brand-new campaign #TogetherForChange. This campaign launched in 2018 is designed specifically to challenge the effects of social media on those who have lost their babies. As I ran my own social media consultancy, Scarletta Media, for nine years - which specialised in social media for business, not only did I have plenty to say about the mechanics of social media and online content, I knew first-hand the changes that needed to be made in order to improve online support for women and men following miscarriage. And my brother-in-law Wayne continues to raise funds for Tommy's by regularly hosting 'bacon butty' breakfasts at his work.

Gradually things are beginning to shift for the better, all these seemingly small actions in isolation accumulate to add up to something greater and far bigger. They gain traction and a wave of momentum. One person alone feels powerless to change anything single-handedly. But put together a collective group of brave and courageous souls willing to take action and make their voices heard and stand up and be seen, and suddenly you find miraculously positive and much-needed change occurs that benefits and heals us all. As people stand collectively together and openly support one another, human kindness, courage and healing prevails.

CHAPTER 13

THE WARMTH IN YOUR HEART
GIVING YOU COURAGE IS GRACE

Writing had become another form of therapy for me. Every day I as soon as I got out of bed, I'd head downstairs make some tea and sit and write my morning pages. Morning pages are ideal for getting all the jumbled thoughts out of your head and down onto the page. You write for a minimum of three or four pages, even if you feel you have nothing to say. Eventually the words consciously flow and you get down what needs to be expressed without holding back or restraint. I had been writing morning pages for several years before my miscarriage, but afterwards they became another lifeline. I couldn't always articulate my feelings out loud, and sometimes I didn't want to tell anyone my dark and depressing thoughts, so my journal became a much-needed safe space to go to at any time of day.

I sensed everything written within my journals would serve another purpose, as my words began to take on a deeper life of their own the more I wrote. As we approached the first anniversary of losing Grace it became transparent that my new purpose would include writing our story and publishing a book. I continued to feel so strongly about what I had been through that I committed to writing regularly when anything came up that I instinctively felt needed to be documented. Initially I thought the book would be about my recovery during the year after my miscarriage, but as the months passed there was more learning and understanding that came to light. I understood that it was imperative to my well-being to take my time with this writing project as I was still immersed in grieving and healing. Focusing on myself first had to be my priority before I opened up fully elsewhere. But still, my inner guidance and whispers spoke loud and clear and gave me nudges that I noticed and acted on, along the lines of:

'We are not done yet. Focus on this subject next. Talk to this person now. Find out more about this topic. Read this blog post. Order this book. Do some more research. Interview these people. And don't forget to write it all down'.

I opened myself up to being led by a powerful force much greater than my conscious mind, and as I followed the insights and breadcrumbs, I came across an advertisement for a writers' workshop in London, with the publishing firm Hay House. As I clicked on the workshop description to find out more, I noticed Julia Cameron best known for her creative book 'The Artist's Way', would be one of our teachers and guide us with our writing practice throughout the weekend. Julia is well known for something else – morning pages. I had diligently worked through 'The Artist's Way' several years before. Then, I realised there was even more synchronicity, this workshop would take place exactly a year to the day after I'd birthed Grace. For a moment I reconsidered, would I be up to going along? But I decided this was too good an opportunity to miss out on, so quickly booked my ticket before I could change my mind.

As the first day of the weekend workshop arrived, my

husband drove me to the local train station. It was unusually quiet on the roads for a Saturday morning. As we pulled up at a set of traffic lights near the station, there was only us and a van in front waiting at the red light. 'What are the chances of this?' said my husband. As I looked up I noticed the branding on the side of the van, in huge lettering down the sides and on the back doors was 'Grace' and underneath 'Parties'. My instincts seemed to be correct, as once more I sensed Grace's approval and that she would be accompanying me to the writers' workshop too.

It was an insightful weekend and I learned all I needed to know about writing and publishing a book. There were plenty of creative tasks, group work and inspirational tutorials from published authors including Julia Cameron. All attendees were invited to submit their own book proposals as Hay House were offering a book deal. As the weekend drew to a close it dawned on me that if I were to write this book, it needed more time to unfold and evolve. My book could not be rushed, deal or no deal. But attending the writers' weekend gave me some much-needed encouragement and inspiration to continue to document my thoughts and insights as well as another thread to my purpose. I held on to the belief that one day, in the not-so-distant future it would be written and published. But first there was more enlightenment and awakening heading my way.

Repeatedly there seemed to be similar unanswered questions I sought answers to and as I noticed them I'd write them down in my journal over and over again. Specifically on why the subject of miscarriage had been shrouded in secrecy and silence for so long? Where did this taboo originate from? Why was the grief of miscarriage swept aside and ignored? Who instigated this within our society? The frustrating thing with miscarriage is medically not getting any answers at all. Often no one can give you a definitive reason as to why it happened. But regardless I wanted to know why it is still so common, why do some women repeatedly miscarry and yet others seem to breeze through pregnancy without any complications? Is this all down to mother nature, is there nothing we can do, or is there something else that can be done to prevent baby loss?

I understand and accept that when there is something genetically wrong with the baby the body instinctively knows what to do and the pregnancy does not continue. Nature knows best and this is the same for everything on the planet, human or otherwise; it is deemed out of our control. But I failed to accept how the impact of miscarriage has been played down within our culture; surely there is something to aid and alleviate the suffering for so many? Another question that repeatedly popped into my mind was why, in this modern scientific age, are so many western women facing detrimental hormonal issues and struggling with their fertility? Surely there must be a reason, or several.

I set off on an another path craving deeper understanding into the reproductive system and fertility, and as I learned more about the importance of balancing our hormones and monthly cycles something else caught my attention that felt significant and had been completely overlooked within all my notes on how to heal from miscarriage; the *Divine Feminine*.

The *Divine Feminine* is defined as one half of the Universal consciousness enabling creation to occur. The counterpart is the *Sacred Masculine* and both must be in balance. However for thousands of years, the feminine has been silenced and suppressed. So another powerful new path emerged and opened up before me, one that I had never considered before, on how to address the delicate balance between the masculine and feminine energies. Books appeared at the right moment, blog posts captivated my attention and I soaked up all this new insight and information coming towards me like a sponge.

I considered with more depth how to heal myself holistically as a whole female being, with both the masculine and feminine energies in balance and not to treat my symptoms and trauma in isolation. I'd read about the significance of family genetics and the impact of our ancestral lineage, particularly on the maternal side of our families. A huge part of the *Divine Feminine* awakening relates to looking to the past, back into our own family history and knowing and understanding the truths of our grandmothers. As I read this paragraph in a blog I was reading, suddenly everything began to make a lot more sense: 'A lot of female ancestral trauma is carried through the generations from mother to daughter and held in the womb. If you have very painful PMS, fertility problems, or any issues at all around your sacral chakra, then work to heal this area of your body as an absolute priority. This is one of the fastest, most effective and most transformational ways to allow the flow of sacred feminine energy into your life.' Finally, there was a bigger picture and I connected the dots. The females in my family had suffered significant trauma specifically within their wombs. This couldn't just be a coincidence, could it?

During the 1960's and 70's my mum's generation were the first women to be offered the revolutionary contraceptive pill. A synthetic hormone taken to suppress the natural hormonal cycle and prevent unwanted pregnancy. When my parents decided they wanted to have a baby my mum stopped taking the pill. She became pregnant and my sister was born, prematurely. And I was born full-term two years later.

I wondered if there could be long-term repercussions of synthetic hormones on our bodies, well-being and fertility that we don't know about? In addition to the contraceptive pill our food chain is overloaded with hormones that we unwittingly consume and digest via meat and dairy products. No one seems to have a definitive answer on this, yet. With my own gynaecological issues my GP at the time advised the only sensible solution for me was to take a synthetic hormone to suppress the oppressive symptoms of fibroids. She was not interested in getting to the root cause of the issue entirely or taking a more detailed medical history.

My mum began to suffer with severe gynaecological symptoms at the age of forty-one. Eventually she opted to undergo a hysterectomy, as the this was the only option at the time if she wanted to free herself of her debilitating symptoms. No one could give her a definitive answer as to why she was suffering. Removal of her womb was advised as the only remedy. Five years later my mum became seriously ill and had to endure further intensive surgery to remove a large ovarian cyst. This time both ovaries were removed. Again no one could advise on the cause, removal was the only option. Problem solved. But was it?

Going back another generation to my maternal grandmother Dorothy, she lived within a generation of women who were conditioned to be ashamed of their bodies and menstruation. It was deemed shameful and taboo to even discuss women's problems with anyone else. They endured in silence. Therefore she never discussed anything to do with being a woman or menstruation with my mum. It all remained hidden and a subject strictly out of bounds, even with her own daughter.

Whilst in her seventies my grandmother became ill; we'd notice her frequently taking heartburn tablets and she rapidly lost weight. Eventually, she admitted to my mum just how unwell she was. It transpired she had been bleeding down below for some time and it hadn't gone away of its own accord. She believed this was normal, of course for a woman in her seventies to suddenly start bleeding again, it is far from normal.

Following extensive medical tests and scans she received her diagnosis; cancer of her womb. In an attempt to prolong her life she underwent a full hysterectomy.

My beloved nanny had been so afraid of telling anyone about what was happening to her she couldn't speak up. This delay in asking for any help cost her dearly. Why hadn't she been able to say anything sooner? By the time she'd found the courage to tell my mum it was too little, too late. The cancer eventually ravaged her body and she sadly passed away. We were all heartbroken to lose her. I was only sixteen years old at the time.

Now older and wiser I understand a little more about her generation and I only wish she were still alive to share her own story. As I reflect on her situation I am honouring her and her voice here too.

In addition to speaking and writing about the impact of miscarriage, I know the taboos and silence run far deeper into the very fabric and essence of our existence as women. The silence and taboo aren't only for miscarriage, it includes menstruation, pregnancy and even menopause. The pattern of suppression is repeated generation after generation. Women have been totally suppressed in every sense. Our bodies and natural hormonal cycles disrespected and ignored. Our voices silenced and drowned out. Our emotions medicated and our stories hidden and buried within.

Is this where the silence comes from?
Is this where the judgement appeared?
Is this what we have to overcome and bring to light?

Yes.
I believe it is.

We must continue to peel back the layers of suppression and get to the root cause. Women need to feel more empowered to embrace their bodies, femininity and fertility. This is the only way to break the silence and diminish the outdated taboos. And maybe help prevent baby loss now and in the future? Or at the very least offer more loving kindness to support every bereaved mother and father to grieve and heal.

Despite things being more open within my own generation, there is still a long way to go. Fortunately for my sister and I my mum talked about periods and they were not shrouded in secrecy. At school we were taught about menstruation, with what physically happens with our monthlies and that they are a normal bodily function and part of life for women. But we were also taught by society at large that when you have a period, to pretend you're not. Just carry on as normal. As periods are a massive inconvenience and don't get you excused from sports. Or anything else for that matter.

And when it came to our own fertility we were told to avoid getting pregnant at all costs. No one wants to be an unmarried teenage mother, as it is shameful. So we try not to get pregnant and then when we are ready for children can't quite figure out why we are experiencing complications and infertility. It is still deeply subconsciously embedded into our minds – do not get pregnant.

Gradually I put the pieces together and realised there has to be a negative impact from all this social conditioning, meddling and suppression. As women like me are so out of whack with our hormones, out of tune and rhythm with our natural cycles and have no idea about repressed female energy, that is it any wonder we are having to deal with unexplained infertility, recurrent miscarriages, traumatic pregnancy complications and stillbirth. Regardless of the advances in medical research and science.

Somewhere along the line our ancestors, generations of women who came before us, were conditioned to be ashamed of their bodies. To cover up and hide. To never discuss what is naturally meant to happen every month. They were not empowered. They were told to put up and shut up. They even referred to their period as *'The Curse'*. Western women have been alienated from themselves and their femininity for a long time. For centuries and centuries thanks to a system of social structures and oppressive masculine practices. This has another name; it's also known as patriarchy – *the rule of the Father*.

Women in eastern cultures are taught to consider their monthly cycles as a precious, sacred time. The ideal time to retreat and reflect. Menstruation is not shrouded in shame or embarrassment. They learn from a young age how to embrace their feminine aspects and as a result are in tune with their natural cycles and in flow. And most importantly they do not seem to have the detrimental fertility issues that we do.

Slowly and thankfully it seems western women are waking up. Our perspective is changing as the feminine energy is making itself known to us once more. Underneath the layers of social repression and conditioning are whispers of infinite feminine wisdom. We are finding our way forward by reconnecting with more feminine instincts and qualities, which include our intuition, healing, love, kindness, softness, wisdom, unity and a more compassionate way of being. We are focusing inwards turning away from the dominant rule of the father, and bringing things back into a more even balance by connecting with the *Divine Mother*.

The womb is a spiritual centre, an extension of the mother energy especially that of mother earth, we bleed with the cycles of the earth and moon, and the wisdom of our wombs is that of the earth. The womb is the bridge between spirit and matter. Of course, every human is here on planet earth thanks to a womb.

Our wombs hold great wisdom, spiritual and creative power and can be healed from trauma, including miscarriage. Our grandmothers carry fifty percent of their grand-daughters' genes. Therefore I believe that the traumas, emotions and beliefs from my grand-mother have directly impacted me.

If I had learnt about the *Divine Feminine* at the age of sixteen maybe, just maybe my own circumstances would be very different today. Maybe my nanny Dorothy's would have too.

I don't blame my body for my miscarriage, but I wish I had been taught how to show my body love and respect instead of only scrutiny. I wish I had been encouraged to embrace being a woman and everything this entails. I wish I had been told and believed that I am enough, regardless of whether I have children or not. I wish I had known how to trust my extraordinary inner voice of wisdom. Because if I had, then I would have insisted my GP refer me to see a gynaecologist far sooner as my own menstrual symptoms were completely abnormal. My instincts did not let me down, she did.

As the months passed my situation hadn't altered and I will always deeply feel the loss of Grace. But her whispers and gentle guidance provided much needed comfort as well as enabling me to heal, evolve and awaken. This holistic journey began to heal my mind, body and spirit. Over time I'd been guided towards mindfulness, energy healing, homeopathy, our garden and mother nature and of course my own creativity. Bit-by-bit it all moved me slowly through the wretched days, weeks and months of grief and gave me purpose, with the resources and tools to cope.

I barely recognised the woman I'd become; I'd gone from the depths of darkness and despair to somehow finding myself heading upwards once more towards the healing light and living again. Establishing the relationship with myself first and foremost is now my new normal. I recognised as I healed, something else awakening, something that had been suppressed and silenced within me and my ancestors for many years. Lifetimes even. I found out how to reconnect to my own femininity and how to courageously express my own inner voice. I now have a voice that will no longer be silenced.

Connecting more deeply with myself and other women means collectively we heal. This is nothing new, this is an ancient practice from woman-to-woman that is being reactivated. We are all sisters of the same family of women throughout time. By healing our line we heal the line of others. We connect, we share, we grieve, we support, we nurture, we encourage, we grow, we bloom and we transform. Together.

Armed with a more feminine outlook and perspective everything had changed despite all that I had been through. I'd found my new normal and this remarkably transformed my life for the better.

HEALING

What makes a mother? – Author Unknown

I thought of you and closed my eyes and prayed to God today, I asked "What makes a mother?" and I know I heard him say a mother has a baby, this we know is true, but God can you be a mother when your baby is not with you?

Yes you can he replied with confidence in his voice, I give many women babies, when they leave it's not their choice. Some I send for a lifetime and others for the day, and some I send to feel your womb, but there is no need to stay.

I just don't understand this God I want my baby here.

He took a breath and cleared his throat and then I saw I tear, I wish I could show you what your child is doing here…..If you could see your child smile with other children and say, we go to earth to learn our lessons of love and life and fear, but my mummy loved me so much I got to come straight here.

I feel lucky to have a mum who had so much love for me, I learnt my lessons very quickly and my mummy set me free. I miss my mummy oh so much but visit her every day, when she goes to sleep on her pillow is where I lay. I stroke her hair and kiss her cheek and whisper in her ear "mummy please don't be sad today I'm your baby and I'm here".

So you see sweet one, your children are OK. Your babies are here in my home and this is where they will stay.

They'll wait for you with me, until your lessons are through, and on the day that you come home they'll be waiting here for you.

So now you see what makes a mother is the feeling in your heart. It's the love you had so much of right from the very start.

CHAPTER 14

SHARE YOUR GIFTS WITH GRACE

Throughout my life I have taken several courageous leaps of faith. At the time I had no idea of the significance of these actions. As I mentioned earlier, at the tender age of nineteen I packed my bags and headed off to France to work as a holiday representative on a campsite. Until this point I'd led a pretty pampered life at home with my parents. I didn't know how to cook, how to wash my clothes, and I didn't have to worry about paying bills. Needless to say, they were flabbergasted when I announced I had applied to work in France. At the time I had what my dad deemed a good job in a call centre, where I earned a decent wage. I had my own car and there were good prospects for career progression. But I didn't want a sensible job, or a conventional life; instead I craved freedom and desired a fresh start, especially as my heart had been broken by the man who I naively believed was the love of my life. It quickly transpired that he most definitely wasn't.

My dad voiced his opinion and said he'd give me two weeks in France until I'd get fed up and be desperate to return home. But I was a determined young woman and wanted to prove him wrong, so against my parents' wishes and advice I chose to accept the job and made my way to France, having absolutely no idea what lay ahead. Somehow I had a deep inner knowing and sensed all would be OK. This is the first time I can recall trusting my intuition to guide me forward.

After the initial two weeks I made a telephone call home and confirmed to my parents that I hadn't had enough yet and would be sticking with my new job a while longer, therefore not to expect me home any time soon. It turned out that I had made the right choice, as by following my instincts I ended up happily living and working in France on-and-off for four years. Being in France transformed my life for the better. My eyes began to open fully to the world around me, I met and connected with different people that I would never have met if I had stayed at home and most importantly, I became an fully fledged adult and gained much needed independence.

Many years later during his speech on my wedding day, my dad told me and our wedding guests that going to France was the making of me. Embarking on this adventure had altered my perspective and had I not trusted myself or my inner guidance I know my life would have taken a very different path, and not one for the better.

Whilst in my early thirties the opportunity arose for me to take another leap of faith into the unknown. I was immersed in what you could deem a more conventional life and with it came the proper job. I was settled in my home life, recently married and my career path had quickly expanded as I'd found myself immersed in the world of business development, marketing and social media. I earned a reasonable wage, gained valuable experience and skills and had learned a lot but I hated the working environment I'd found myself in. Logically it ticked all the boxes – spiritually it ticked none.

Working for this particular company did not suit me at

all, over time it depleted my spirit and self-confidence. I'd continuously find myself undermined, undervalued and totally unappreciated. Instinctively I knew my days were numbered as I couldn't conform and failed to thrive in a ruthless, alpha-male environment with relentless pressure to deliver day after miserable day. Eventually I reached the point of no return; my tolerance snapped and I knew it was time for me to move on. Fortunately, my husband and family encouraged me to resign even though I didn't have another job to go to.

Once more I took a leap towards an unknown future, but despite the uncertainty I trusted myself enough to go with the flow and figure it out. On reflection I know what cemented my decision to leave and leap again. It was being tasked with making one of my team redundant following the devastating miscarriage of her twins. Before she could attempt to try for another pregnancy she had to go. This was in 2009 - not the stone age. Despite the professional façade, woman to woman we both knew the real reason why she suddenly found her position redundant and it was far from ethical; it was unlawful discrimination. This experience triggered something so profoundly deep within that I have never forgotten it. When this incident occurred I'd been married less than a year and fully expected to start our family imminently. However, I knew never to voice my intention to become a mother to my employer as I fully understood precisely what the business culture was all about. And it wasn't long after I married that I was asked to share more about my baby plans. I chose not to and kept quiet.

On the inside I felt totally incensed and wondered how this appalling discrimination against women could still be happening within the workplace. Hadn't we moved on and evolved? It seemed not and I was aware that it was only a question of time before I too found myself unfairly dismissed, redundant and out of a job before I could become pregnant and a mother.

Despite my longing for motherhood this event planted

the seed inside me that made me realise I never again wanted to work for a business or organisation that chose to treat its staff, particularly women, so badly.

After I left this job, we retreated to France for a much-needed holiday. Being in France always works its magic on me; I feel as though I am at home, in my rightful place, and since we married my husband and I visit at least once a year. Fortunately, he now loves France as much as I do. During our holiday I had the time and space to reflect and reinvigorate body, mind and soul resulting in something within my creativity beginning to spark. Whilst in France I decided to write and create my own blog, 'Scarletta's Blog' where I could share everything I'd learned and experienced about the social media revolution. I returned home with a renewed sense of purpose and direction. I followed the breadcrumbs and embraced a new way of being and working, for myself.

Saying yes to this new endeavour meant it wasn't long before another exciting door flew open and my blog evolved into my own small business; a social media marketing consultancy for small, or as I referred to them, petite businesses, I called it 'Scarletta Media'. It was remarkable that as my petite business grew and flourished I did too. My intention was to establish my own business that would enable me to continue to work and support our family going forward. Listening to and trusting my inner guidance served me well. Miraculously I'd found myself in the right place at the right time, as thanks to the social media revolution my business and I blossomed and evolved organically as I taught other business owners how to use social media to market their businesses. Even though I'd never aspired to become an entrepreneur, my world elevated. I met and connected with many inspirational women and loved my work and freedom. Being based predominantly online meant plenty of opportunities to work with clients all over the world - all thanks to the internet.

After several years I established more of a niche market by being a *Social Media Stylist*, encouraging women in business to create more of an authentic, living brand by stepping forward and being more visible within their business brand identity and message. You could say I was riding the wave to success.

The world of business began to shift and change, especially for women. It is true what they say, often you'll end up teaching precisely what you need to be reminded of yourself. Time after time I'd meet and work with women who had had enough of being ignored, overlooked and silenced. I'd hear stories of women leaving the corporate world, disillusioned and deflated because their skills and expertise were not enough. They were not receiving equal pay and if they dared to step off the career ladder to have children, on their return from maternity leave they found themselves demoted into part-time roles with part-time money but a full-time workload. Once again I wondered how this could still be happening in our modern and forward-thinking lifetime.

As I approached my forties, professionally I felt creatively stifled and disillusioned with the world of social media, which had become a noisy and intrusive place. I refused to play the marketing popularity game or adhere to the advertising tricks and tactics in order to be seen or heard. This meant instead of continuing to grow and expand, despite my best intentions I began to shrink. Suddenly my world got smaller, I no longer felt as bold or courageous, I felt increasingly anxious and afraid. I would find myself saying 'no' more than saying 'yes'. As my confidence and self-belief began to tumble, I retreated into my shell.

I knew things needed to change, but I no longer had the inner strength or energy to take action. I had no idea what I needed to do to get myself out of this funk. For the first time ever I could not take a leap anywhere as I did not know where to go whilst feeling so lost and confused. My life felt meaningless and trivial; worthless even. Everything seemed to be closing in around me, I felt claustrophobic and I couldn't get on the Tube in London without panicking that something dreadful was about to happen. I had a panic attack on a flight to Greece; I'd always loved travelling but began to dread it. This sense of darkness and doom seemed to be in the driving seat of my entire life, everything suffered as a result and I was terrified of the future.

Somehow and somewhere I'd lost faith in my life and myself. Was my quest to become a mother at the core of this anxiety? Maybe it was. Or was it the repercussions of feeling a total failure? Maybe it was this too. Whatever it was it hit me hard. Typically I am a positive person, always seeing the cup half-full instead of half-empty. But not this time. I knew I had tipped head-first into a mid-life crisis and at the core of this deep unhappiness was my own self-worth and identity. And this all began to unravel before my miscarriage with Grace.

My interest in spirituality continued to offer some guidance and an alternative way of thinking and being in the world. The more I learned and absorbed, the more I felt drawn to weave my own insights, observations and beliefs into my work and business. I would write about how I perceived that women were changing in life and business, that we were connecting with our own voices and finding a way to speak up more about what we felt and believed needed to change. We wanted to feel empowered and have freedom of expression and autonomy. Powerful stories were being shared online and off, and this was the beginning of a much-needed shift and more feminine awakening and evolution that would eventually include my own.

I had simply outgrown my Scarletta business and desperately wanted to let go of the work, brand and identity and emerge fully in my own right. But something continued to niggle away at me, I sensed the timing was off, something did not sit comfortably within and my intuition urged me to wait a little longer. I am not a patient person at the best of times as when I set my mind to doing something I give it my all. I do not like to wait for anything yet this time I had no other option and felt compelled to wait.

Gently my work and services evolved naturally and firmly under the radar. Instinctively I'd find myself offering deeper, heart-felt personal development work with my clients where everything was led by more feminine instincts and intuition; way over and above a typical logical business strategy. As I connected with more and more like-minded spiritual women, I knew it wouldn't be too much longer before I felt able to take my next leap of faith, but still things weren't clear, and I needed more clarity. For the first time in my life I slowed down and waited patiently, however uncomfortable and frustrating this felt. Thank goodness I did because I had absolutely no idea what lay ahead. Just as I felt another leap coming my way for my career and business, I became pregnant with Grace. And following the miscarriage, everything, including my petite business, began to crumble to the ground.

Losing Grace became an unexpected but much needed catalyst for transformational change both personally and professionally. Truthfully I'd felt disillusioned with my life long before we lost her, but this feeling only intensified afterwards. I found a way to keep things ticking over and met any existing obligations to clients, but I knew my heart was no longer in it. I'd come to the very edge of my entire life and there was absolutely no room anymore for anything superficial or meaningless. I was prepared to walk away from everything and start all over again – I knew the phoenix would rise from the ashes but all in her own good time.

In the year following my miscarriage I worked from home, pottered in the garden and did what I had to do with no idea where to head next; there was no sense of purpose or direction to speak of. Everything felt like a jumble in my mind. Brené Brown refers to this as a 'Midlife Unravelling'. This was mine.

By the time eighteen months had passed, spring was emerging and I knew the time had come for me to emerge as well and start living fully again I needed to kick-start my career. I couldn't remain in the depths of grief forever drifting through each day indefinitely, it wasn't doing my confidence or self-esteem any good by remaining at home alone all the time. So I plucked up the courage to head back into London and started to network again. Fortunately, a community meet-up designed specifically for soulful business owners had restarted and fortuitously it was here where fate played a hand and ensured I met someone very special, my wonderful friend Hayley.

At the time Hayley and I met we were both busy talking to other people deeply engrossed in conversation, but despite this a persistent voice in my head interrupted my chatter and instructed me to speak with the woman wearing red in front of me, that being Hayley. As I did, I introduced myself and said: 'for some reason I feel compelled to speak to you'. Fortunately Hayley didn't run away thinking I was completely nuts and we had a lovely chat about what we both do and swapped business cards.

What I hadn't known at the time was that Hayley was a gifted intuitive healer and offered 'Soul Plan' readings. The 'Soul Plan' is based on ancient text which helps you become realigned with your soul's purpose to gain a greater sense of being and life satisfaction. Your 'Soul Plan' enables you to connect with your true purpose, drawn from your life experiences that provide the greatest learning, expansion and joy and each plan is derived from quantum physics and ancient Hebrew numerology. The 'Soul Plan' could reveal a potential new career direction or help gain clarity on the powerful lessons behind the areas where you experience suffering or challenges in life.

Having spent a considerable amount of time immersed in the void, the unknown and uncertain space that sits in between here and there, with no idea what to do next, I was an ideal client for the 'Soul Plan'. I felt totally dissatisfied with my life, longed for a sense of purpose and it seemed that no matter how hard I tried to take steps forward I continued to feel stuck. I was intrigued to learn more about the 'Soul Plan' readings and trusted that Hayley was the ideal person to help me find clarity. Remarkably she felt I could help her too, so we became each other's client and quickly got to know each other well and became firm friends.

Prior to meeting Hayley again in London for my 'Soul Plan' reading I wondered what would come up. What was I destined to do for the rest of my days? Was anything significant repeatedly happening in my life and why?

I deliberately hadn't mentioned Grace or my miscarriage to Hayley. When we'd spoken it had always been work-related so it took us both by surprise during our reading when she told me that she had channeled a specific message for me. It didn't make a lot of sense to her, but she said maybe it would for me:

'As I honour my connection with the earth and my emotions, I allow the Grace of spirit to run through me and touch the lives of many. My goal is to be the catalyst to help others see who they truly are. And so it is.'

Hayley asked me: 'Who is Grace?'. I told her and explained the significance of this message. We were both stunned. Yet again Grace was lighting my path ahead.

I began to cry; this message definitely made total sense to me. It was what I had come to realise myself but needed some sort of divine intervention to make me believe I was capable of doing this work.

Following our initial session Hayley sent me a copy of my 'Soul Plan' and contained within was the guidance I desperately needed to hear. There were three significant things that were highlighted within my plan and what my soul intended for me to learn and grow from during this lifetime. Firstly about my practical and down to earth energy which helps me tap into my own inner wisdom and intuition. Secondly the theme of life and death featured strongly, which I had to learn and overcome through the tragic loss of Grace and finally how I could choose to use the strength of my own resilience to help comfort and support others following loss. Hayley reaffirmed how everything has a higher meaning and Grace's passing would have been a path that she chose for various reasons and one that would have been to help me and my family grow at a deeper, soul-level and come to a greater level of acceptance of life and death.

At this very moment something sparked deep within my soul. I knew my destiny was to encourage and empower women to reconnect with themselves, with their inner knowing, intuition and wisdom; to use their own voices and embrace their freedom. And also to support women during significant life transitions, such as bereavement, divorce, redundancy, illness or their own mid-life awakening. This was at the heart and soul of my work all along and it had been re-enforced during the loss of Grace and in the depths of my grief. I was awakening to a renewed sense of purpose and service. My work was not separate from me or my quest to voice the impact of miscarriage – it was all meant to become entwined; as one.

For the first time in a long time the dark fog surrounding me began to lift. Finally I could look back and see how every thread of my life and work so far meant something meaningful. Nothing was wasted, everything was and is significant, including the loss of Grace. I would never get my answer as to why we lost her. My friend was wrong when she said I'd eventually find a gift in our loss. There is no gift in losing your much-longed-for baby, but there is meaning; eventually you find and stumble upon meaning and a renewed sense of purpose and direction that comes from your heart and soul.

Armed with my 'Soul Plan' and intuitive guidance from Hayley I embarked on another new chapter in my life, this time there wasn't a huge leap into the unknown, just a more delicate step forward. As I did so life began to transform around me and I took my first steps out of the depths of the void.

Several weeks later Hayley and I met again, this time for us to work together on her business. During our lunch break Hayley surprised me with a gift. I opened the parcel and wrapped in beautiful paper was a stone, etched with gold letters - Grace. I looked at the stone and back up at Hayley; this was an amazing gift. She had recently bumped into one of her friends who said she had something for her and would instinctively know who the person was for whom it was intended. Of course Hayley knew immediately this was destined for me. I am full of gratitude for my Grace stone and knew yet again our Grace Rose was enticing and encouraging me forward. Thanks to Hayley's guidance and encouragement I had my plan, a plan that is within my destiny and of course includes and is guided by my beloved angel Grace.

As for my treasured Grace stone, it sits proudly on my desk and serves as a daily reminder for me to always remember who I am, what I am here to do and how I have to keep finding the courage to share my gifts with Grace, just in case I should lose sight of my soul purpose ever again.

CHAPTER 15

EXPRESS YOURSELF WITH EASE AND GRACE

The continuous thread of bringing women together became more and more prominent in my life and work, not only with regards to using our voices for a good cause and to share our wisdom, but also to give ourselves permission to show up more powerfully with vulnerability and authenticity. I realised I have always been a confidante, friends or even people I have never met before will open up and tell me their innermost thoughts and over the years I've frequently found myself being a trusted keeper of stories and secrets.

Following the loss of Grace these deep and meaningful conversations began to happen with rapid frequency. Only the conversations and storytelling weren't always about others needing to off-load their inner-most thoughts, sometimes someone would share a nugget of wisdom with me that was precisely what I needed to know in the moment. They'd gift me an insight, a piece of wisdom, share necessary guidance, reaffirm something, tell me with absolute clarity that I am on the right track and pretty much tell me the next step I needed to take. All I had to do was commit and take action. As the weeks and months passed, I continually felt guided and supported by a miraculous life force.

I continued to operate and offer my services within my Scarletta business brand and personally was asked to contribute and share my own insights regarding my miscarriage and the loss of Grace. I sat on forums and discussed the impact of baby loss and made my own contribution regarding our experience and insights. My friend Lesley was in the midst of writing her first book – 'Finding Joy Beyond Childlessness' and we'd have many conversations about the importance of telling our own stories. So much so Lesley asked me if I'd be willing to be a contributor to her book and write a section sharing my own story and how writing supported me through the trauma and enabled me to move forward through the path to grieving and healing.

I also worked with Jo Tocher, a miscarriage mentor and well-being practitioner from 'Life After Miscarriage'. The one-to-one sessions with Jo were fantastic and allowed me to work with my emotions, release the pent-up energy and share what I really felt, all in a safe space. Once again I became a contributor to another much-needed book. Jo wrote and published "Life After Miscarriage – Your guide to healing from pregnancy loss" and included within was our story with Grace. I was willing and open to sharing my own story and using my voice if it helped someone else in need.

Gradually my work and calling became entwined. I felt deeply passionate and compelled to help women and it was no longer only about supporting them and being a confidante in a work capacity or personally through loss; my purpose and role was about being there to encourage women to transform in their entirety.

For a long time I had deliberated whether or not to create my own group for women. My idea had bubbled away for several years. I had pages and pages of notes within my ideas notebook. This group was all about connection, deeper conversation, honesty, encouragement and collective growth for women.

It wasn't about what we do, it had everything to do with who we really are, underneath the layers of social conditioning and job titles. Specifically, what shaped us, our fears, dreams and goals; our big life intentions and our real purpose and meaning. I knew that when women come together something remarkable occurs. We could encourage each other to show up authentically in the world and make our difference. Somehow.

I heard this call repeatedly. I knew in my heart and soul I had to create this and yet I felt afraid. What if I had got it wrong? What if no other woman felt as I did? What if I failed and no one joined me? Did I really need to put myself, my story and my voice out there within my business? I didn't know the answers to any of these questions so I chose to do nothing. I'd had enough to deal with in my personal life and as I was only just feeling a little more positive about life, so I decided to park this idea for the time being.

Yet my idea would not go away. During a meditation session I could see myself standing by the ocean. Then as I stood transfixed by the horizon something deeply profound occurred in my mind's-eye. One-by-one women stepped forward and joined me as we stood together in a line. No one was further forward and no one was behind, all of us stood together collectively in solidarity. This vision became a frequent visitor. My inner voice continued to share its frustration and opinions – such as did other women see that we were still being ignored and our voices suppressed? Did they know that we had to support and encourage each other if anything was going to improve and change for the better? Surely there were others out there who felt as strongly as I did about miscarriage, emotional health and well-being, equality and a more feminine way of life.

It transpired there were. Unbeknown to me I was about to meet another special woman in my local supermarket and have a conversation that would change how I went about my work and business. Whilst standing in the queue, an elderly man on a mobility scooter was in front of me. He paid for his shopping and made off to leave but accidentally hit the power on his scooter too hard. He ended up crashing into a bench located on the other side of the aisle. We all laughed. (He was OK; I really don't just go around laughing at the misdemeanors of elderly men on their scooters!). The lovely checkout lady said: "You can have my L plates, as I have just passed my driving test". We laughed some more and fortunately he made it out of the shop unscathed. I began to pack my shopping and said to her how brilliant it was that she'd passed her driving test and freedom beckoned. Suddenly the conversation took a more serious tone. She looked up at me and said: "If only".

With tears in her eyes she shared that she had spent the last eight years trying to learn how to drive. Now that she had passed her test her husband wouldn't allow her to use the car. He didn't want her to drive herself anywhere without him. He had to know exactly what she was doing and with whom at all times. She went on to explain that in her culture you do not disobey your husband. And yet here she was in a country surrounded by women with opportunities and their freedom. Why couldn't she have the same?

In that moment I saw her. Really saw her. I could immediately sense what she was not saying aloud. Something profound passed between us. She continued to say that since moving to the UK she was more unhappy than she'd ever been. Because her freedom had been taken away. Before she moved here and married her husband she was free, but now she wasn't. This was not the life her mother had intended for her and she had decided it was too late to change. But she would do everything in her power to ensure her young daughter's life would be very different than her own. I nodded. I heard her. I understood. I felt her pain and anguish. I wished her life was different too.

She asked me what I do. I told her that I am fortunate to have my freedom. That I am able to work with brilliant women who have theirs too. Some have their own businesses; many are on a powerful mission or they may use their voice to share their stories. Or they may even want to do something more meaningful but are not sure how. So I help them. To be the change that many of us desperately wish to see in our lifetime. What she said next stayed with me. She told me that I must do everything I can to help the women around me. To embrace my freedom. To speak up on her behalf. To do what I can for those who for whatever reason cannot. I promised her I would. I also told her that it is never too late for her to change her life for the better. She deserved to be happy and she was just as entitled to her freedom as I was. I left the shop and drove home with a heavy heart and tears falling down my face. How could this still be happening to women in our lifetime? But the sad truth is it is and a lot more.

I knew it was time for me to follow her advice. She had given me a powerful insight. I'd met her for a reason. Every time I go into the supermarket I look for her. But I have never seen her since. If ever I needed a sign or a nudge or a monumental kick up the arse from the Universe, the powers that be or whatever you choose to call it; THIS was it. Instinctively I knew what I had to do. I had to get out of my own way and trust and believe that what I saw and felt, others did too. It was time for this idea of mine to become a reality. There was nothing to stop me except my own doubts and fears.

Two years after the miscarriage I found myself creating and launching another new endeavour, a unique and exclusive group for women – The Social Collective - and this was all thanks to a heartfelt conversation I had with a brave and courageous woman who trusted me enough to tell me her story.

I put my fears to one side and waited to see what would happen. It didn't take long before one-by-one remarkable women signed up to join me in the Collective. Over the last eighteen months all of us have collectively transformed ourselves, our lives and businesses for the better. I lead and facilitate our group and we have found ourselves part of something special together. All these incredible women have been with me supporting and encouraging me forwards too.

I am eternally grateful to the angel in the supermarket and the women who are and have been in my collective and within my support community. The 'Social Collective' is for all women. Soulful women. Women on a mission. Women who know they are capable of more. Women who have their freedom of speech. Women who know they have something important to share. Women who want to serve. Women who want to empower others. Women who have something important to do. Women who are brave, courageous and sometimes afraid. Women who are willing to be vulnerable and share their stories in order to help others in their time of need. Women who are willing to readdress the balance between the masculine and feminine. Women who say: 'we've had enough of being ignored, overlooked, suppressed and belittled'. Women who simply are THE change.

Why did I create it? Because I could. I promised the angel lady in the supermarket that I would. For her and her daughter. For me and for my beloved Grace. For my beautiful nieces. For all the women who are willing to be the change. Even more so for those around us who cannot be.

It's for all of us. Because things MUST change. Don't they? The Dalai Lama said that the world will be saved by the western woman. I realise this is not because we are the only ones with insightful wisdom or magical feminine powers. It's because we have more freedom than others. We have the tools ready and waiting at our disposal. We can express our voices to speak our truth. We are stepping forward and rising so others can see and hear us. We have absolutely nothing to fear. Not anymore. But we must make the choice. Are we all in? Or out?

For me – I was definitely all IN and realised there is a far bigger and more meaningful job for me to do and armed with this insight I had a brand new business to create.

And finally could take my next leap into the future as I courageously began to express myself with more ease and grace.

CHAPTER 16

GROW, BLOOM AND TRANSFORM
WITH GRACE

At the beginning of 2018 I created a 'vision book'. Instead of having a vision board on my office wall filled with inspirational images and things I wanted to manifest, I chose to fill an entire notebook for the coming year ahead. Contained within were quotes I loved, positive little reminders to perk me up, magical moments that occurred during my day, actions I'd taken, gorgeous images cut out from magazines that deeply resonated and my own important intentions, actions and progress. Everything was contained in one place where I could add to it quickly and easily as well as review and reflect.

Whenever I drifted off course, or the negative committee in my head told me I hadn't done enough, or someone else wanted me to put their intentions and priorities before my own I paused for a moment. I picked up the notebook, flicked through the pages and suddenly returned to a place of positivity. My mindset shifted; I felt inspired and encouraged. I reconnected with myself and focused once more. And there was always an inner nudge that whispered: 'This is what YOU intend to do, remember?'

But as well as keeping me focused, productive and on track, this magical notebook enabled miracles. The words and images took on a life of their own. To someone else my notebook may have looked meaningless. However to me it became precious and full of meaning. Because adding to my vision book meant something remarkable happened. One of my biggest transformations occurred. An epiphany of sorts. What I hadn't envisaged was that over time, season by season and month by month as the content on the pages grew, something was beginning to bloom. To grow and transform right before my eyes.

It was quite a moment when I realised what I had unintentionally created. Because it was glaringly obvious when I could see everything together staring back at me from the carefully crafted pages. Suddenly as if by magic all the answers I had been seeking for a long time were right there. Beautifully contained within my magical notebook. Everything that mattered to me and what really lights me up.

As I added to the book during the first six months of the year, as I flicked through the pages it reflected back everything about me, the woman I've become and who I am now. And this cemented how I intended to show up and live my own life. It was all there. This realisation meant finally I could connect the dots. I'd found the clarity I'd been seeking for my purpose going forwards and armed with this insight I began to create my new business, brand identity and website.

At the core of my new business I could clearly see myself working with individuals and groups of women to encourage them to make themselves a priority in their lives and work. To learn how to reconnect and get reacquainted with the woman within, just as I had learned to do since my miscarriage. I trusted and believed that my soul purpose going forward is centred on supporting and mentoring women to reconnect to their divine femininity and intuition. I wanted to empower them to use their voices for change and a new addition to my consultancy services was to show women how to immerse themselves in the great outdoors and use mother earth to support their healing and awakening.

The pages of my vision book demonstrated what truly mattered to me and I could see that it was all there beautifully waiting for me to notice and let go of the past, move further out of the void and fully embrace the new. Unconsciously I had documented everything I needed and so I got to work and within the space of three weeks I had designed, created and launched a new business and website filled with my words and photo images. A new logo was created with my own name in a gold font and gorgeous flowers sat above my name in the colours of the 'Grace' and 'Amazing Grace' roses. Everything was intentional and deliberate. Our garden had been my go-to sanctuary where being amongst the trees and wildlife had given me much needed wisdom to reconnect me to my intuitive self, so the seasons, life cycles and mother earth were prominent within my new brand.

My first business brand had flowers and so it felt as though almost ten years on I'd come full circle. I went back to the beginning once more and allowed myself the freedom to create with a blank canvas and relished the opportunity to start all over again without any 'shoulds' or 'must dos'; I followed whatever felt right. The fabulous women within the 'Social Collective' gave me their honest and open feedback about how we all worked together and this is how I became a transformational mentor because this is precisely what I had been doing for quite some time and all of them re-enforced how I had encouraged and enabled them to transform from within. My new services boldly announced the heartfelt one-to-one discovery-of-self mentoring programmes available and of course the 'Social Collective' with the overall purpose of my work being about growing, blooming and transforming.

As I wrote my new about page, I felt it was essential to include a little about my own midlife unravelling, or as I now refer to it - my own graceful awakening. I alluded to my own miscarriage story and talked about Grace Rose, what had changed in my own life and my purpose going forward and why.

A friend commented on my bravery and boldness at daring to mention my miscarriage within my business website, 'Shouldn't you keep them separate?', she said. 'Do you really want people to know everything about you?'. Bravery, being bold and daring - three powerful words that I completely related to. But I would not be shamed into leaving Grace out of my life story as I recognised this would be disempowering. There was absolutely no way I could be truly authentic if I was not willing to share and speak the truth about my own loss. How could I teach or lead by example if I chickened out and hid my own truth silenced in shame? How could I continue to honour Grace if I felt ashamed or embarrassed to talk about her in person or online?

I was under no illusion that being bold would make others recoil and many would prefer I'd kept Grace to myself. But I was far enough into my own entrepreneurial journey to know that you aren't for everyone and I fully expected some who had once been in my tribe and community to disappear the moment I dared to mention the word miscarriage. I trusted that those who wanted to stay would and those who didn't would move on to someone else instead. I couldn't pretend to be anything else other than who I am and the only way to be the change is by being open, honest and transparent about my own story. Not just selectively sharing the best bits. But all of it.

I knew in my heart and soul precisely what I had to do. With my work and business going forward my clients and community would see, hear and experience all of me. Not just the show-reel. All of me. The truth. The vulnerability. The power. The discomfort. The darkness. The light. The joy. All of it. Because this is what true authenticity and whole-hearted living and being truly means. When I hit publish on my new website it felt liberating. I'd been in the void for a couple of years and suddenly everything clicked into place and felt absolutely right and in true alignment with the real woman I'd become.

I also felt it pertinent to be honest and open with the truth as I had been asked to participate and share our story for a new television documentary about the silence surrounding miscarriage. When faced with an important decision to make I usually follow my 'yes', 'no' or 'maybe' gut instinct and in this case it was an immediate 'yes'. But I knew participating was going to be tough. I am used to being in front of the camera. I can talk for England about topics I feel passionately about. I know how to use my social platform as a force for good as best I can. Yet being in front of the camera talking about the loss of our precious baby Grace Rose was going to be my biggest challenge and test me to my core.

Despite my vulnerability, often the overwhelming desire to do whatever I can eventually kicks in. My mission for my life and soul-led work became more transparent so the only option was to say 'yes' to using my voice to speak out about what I feel must change. Now I say 'yes' to sharing my input and feedback on new campaigns to help raise awareness. I say 'yes' to fully showing up and offering support to others who've lost their babies. I'll continue to do all of this and more even though sometimes I'd prefer to hide away and stay quiet.

The biggest transformation since losing Grace is that I am willing to step up and be the change I wish to see in the world. Which means these days I often find myself totally out of my comfort zone agreeing to do things that would be easier for me to say no to, such as commenting on blogs, contributing to books, being interviewed for podcasts and participating in a documentary. But when I find my courage and say 'yes' maybe, just maybe my input or action will help someone else in their time of need.

A week or so before our filming date, I had a change of heart. I asked myself if I really wanted to do this? Did I really want to share my story openly on camera? Wouldn't it be easier to let someone else share theirs instead?

Because when you're talking about an emotive subject like losing your baby there is still stigma. I know people who haven't experienced a loss like ours would prefer it if I said nothing, got on with it and kept quiet. As sharing what happened often makes them feel uncomfortable. Talking it over with my husband helped me find my courage and the clarity I needed to participate. I agreed to go along and be interviewed and headed off to a nearby hotel to meet with the presenter and the crew.

The documentary was called 'Silent Loss Hidden Truth of Miscarriage'. The interview was tough going and it stirred up a lot of memories and deeply held emotions. More makeup was needed halfway through as the tears arrived in abundance, but we got there in the end and I felt I had expressed exactly what I needed to. Afterwards I felt completely emotionally drained, so I headed home to spend some quiet time with my husband, reflecting and remembering my reasons for doing it and that I'd agreed to do this for Grace and us. I'd also done it for the other parents-to-be who continue to suffer in silence. I hoped and trusted I had done my bit and made us all proud.

One person cannot change the entire world, but we can all do what we can. It's easy to sit back and believe someone else can speak up on our behalf. Someone else will make the necessary changes. Someone else will bravely share their story and that will be enough to see the change we wish to see. But why not me? Why not you? Why should someone else do it on our behalf? Maybe you wonder whether you and you alone can make any impact? Whether anyone else cares about what you have to say? Whether anyone is interested and would listen? The answer is always yes. Somebody somewhere always benefits. We can all go and hide if we choose to. But if something truly matters to you, you will choose to do something about it. You will do whatever you can. You will find a way forward.

As a result of our collective voices rising, things are beginning to change for the better and gain momentum. People are now willing to have the tough conversations about all sorts of emotive subjects. We are learning about the benefits of opening up and sharing our stories. We understand more about the impact of loss on our emotional and mental health. We are seeing the positive impact of connection, community and support. As a result, people are feeling less isolated and alone.

Several months after filming, the documentary was ready to be viewed at a special screening in a small cinema in London. We decided to go along alone without our families and friends as we had to see it first without worrying about them being upset as well as ourselves.

On the morning of the screening as I opened the curtains at home I looked outside into the garden only to be greeted with the most beautiful rainbow and a little white feather falling from the sky on the other side of the window. 'Hello Grace', I whispered. I knew and trusted she was giving me a sign that she would be accompanying us to the documentary screening too.

We arrived at the venue and took our seats at the back. I felt anxious about watching myself talking about Grace on the screen. It is not easy to watch yourself so distraught and upset, reliving something you'd rather forget. It was fortunate it was dark because as soon as the documentary began, so did our tears. With my husband at my side we sat huddled together; we feel the loss differently, but Grace will always be ours. Our shared loss and our beloved angel.

I needn't have worried as the documentary had been

beautifully put together and featured our story along with a few others. I could never have envisaged participating in something like this a few years before and everything resonated especially regarding the importance of having the impact and trauma of miscarriage acknowledged and supported.

At the end of the screening during the Q&A session, I decided to stand up and say a few words. I didn't know who the other members of the audience were, but this was an opportunity to share just how important it was for all of us to have our stories heard and how I hoped this documentary would enlighten others in order to bring about important change for the better surrounding the silence and isolation around miscarriage and baby loss.

Afterwards we made our way back home, another layer of grieving and healing had been released. I'd turned a corner but felt totally drained and wrung out. This documentary had been on my radar for several months and it took every ounce of strength to show up and do my bit.

When back at home my husband told me how proud he was of me. I felt relieved; a huge weight lifted off my shoulders. I felt immense pride too and proud that instead of keeping quiet I'd spoken up. Proud that despite the vulnerability I'd shared our story openly. Proud that I found the inner strength and resilience to talk about our baby daughter and the fact that she will never be forgotten. Proud that I'd survived and somehow thrived despite hitting rock bottom. And proud of knowing that despite what anyone else may think or say I am and always will be Grace's mother. I hoped I had made Grace proud too.

It wasn't long before another opportunity arose for me to speak my truth, this time I was asked to be a guest speaker at an event in London to talk about my own transformational story and work. Again I said 'yes', before I could say 'no'. Despite feeling apprehensive and nervous beforehand, this was the first time I stepped up in my entirety as me and talked about how my entire life, work and business changed forever following the loss of our daughter Grace Rose.

On the day there were over forty businesses women in the room waiting for me to begin. As I uttered my first few words I could feel my voice quiver. No one knew in advance what I planned to say. I had an inkling but simply stood in front of the audience and spoke from my heart to theirs.

To this day I have no idea what I said exactly, but I recall the room being so quiet you could hear a pin drop. The words flowed through me and when I stopped talking I looked around the room and could see forty pairs of eyes staring back at me. What had just happened? It was unlike anything I'd ever experienced before. As I returned to my seat the applause continued and afterwards several of the women came up to me and gave me a hug. One told me I was an inspiration. Another told me she'd lost her baby too. Miraculously I had found a way to connect on a deep heart-felt level with these women in the room. There was no judgement only support and encouragement. It is what I believe us women do best. Support and empower each other when sharing our wisdom.

Yet again, despite my vulnerability I was willing to show up and do what I felt was necessary. During my talk I said that at the heart and centre of my work today is my own voice, wisdom and story. I stood before them with nothing but the whole truth. With me what you see is what you get and now I have awakened I will never be silenced.

One of the on-going challenges I witness women trying to overcome, is denial. We are conditioned to ignore our miscarriage, forget it or deny it ever happened. Pretend all is well, even if it isn't. The denial of the true impact of miscarriage does nothing to alter or change the silence or taboo. Women are suppressing their heartache, grief, emotions, thoughts and feelings because they believe they should. In order to change the suppression, the discussion should not only include how frequently miscarriages happen, but precisely what happens and how to deal and cope with the aftermath.

Now it is our time, to collectively stand together in solidarity and use our voices and wisdom to unashamedly embrace everything about being a woman. This includes our bodies, minds and souls, our divine feminine skills and qualities, our creativity, emotions and inherent inner wisdom. And we must be courageous and willing to talk and open up about the hard and dark stuff too, especially the loss of our babies.

We owe it to ourselves, our daughters, sisters, mothers, grand-mothers and all of those who came before us to do whatever we can. As this is the only way we begin to change the future for all the women and our soul-sisters who will come after us.

Change begins and gains momentum with each and every woman being willing to acknowledge their own suffering and speak of their loss, heartache and grief with transparency and vulnerability despite the shame and judgement that may arise. We must pass the knowledge and understanding on. Only by doing so will it encourage and empower other women to feel able to do the same. I believe this is the only way the silence and taboo that surrounds miscarriage will diminish once and for all.

CHAPTER 17

THE POWER OF DIVINE GRACE IS WITHIN YOU

As we get to the end of any story we always hope for a happy ending and I would love to say everything is better, that I have my happy ending and am healed and filled with hope and optimism. But truthfully, from my experience, grief never ends. It sometimes swirls in my mind and makes its presence known as I experience the highs and lows of navigating my life. There are plenty of moments where I wonder how on earth I can contemplate living the rest of my life without my children, or even my own grand-children? The overwhelming sadness and crippling heartache can knock me firmly back into the paralysing darkness. But eventually, in time, it passes and shifts, and I feel more comfortable confronting my fears and moving through them with self-compassion and kindness rather than opting to ignore my thoughts or avoid how I really feel. The choice is mine - to continue to work on taking each day as it comes and not to dwell too much on the past or future, just focus on the now.

I hold on to the fact that even though Grace did not make it into the physical world I will always be her mother. I cherish the weeks we were together during my pregnancy. I know what it feels like to bond with your own child as I continue to experience an unbreakable loving connection that is infinite. And no one can take this away from me. The loss of Grace changed everything in my life and went on to bring me many unexpected gifts and insights. Especially around acceptance of myself as a person that regardless of me bringing a baby into this world I am enough. As a woman in her own right I am enough. As a wife, daughter, sister, auntie, friend or acquaintance - I am enough. As I am.

If more women stood together in solidarity and supported and encouraged each other, whatever our life circumstances around motherhood I am sure the world would quickly transform into a much better, more compassionate empowered place and the silence and taboo would eventually recede.

I practice gratitude as best I can, to remind myself and appreciate what is wonderful in my life and the loving support I have around me. Meditation, writing and of course being outdoors immersed in nature and tending to my garden are my constant go-to therapies. They all continue to be cathartic tools to support my physical, mental and emotional well-being and come highly recommended for coping and dealing with everything life has to throw at us.

Despite my best intentions I could not heal alone and the one-to-one coaching energy therapy with Jo Tocher and hypnotherapy sessions, enabled me to release the trauma and significantly reduce the impact of post-traumatic stress. Having hypnosis also enabled me to face another big fear and I managed to fly to the other side of the world for my sister-in-law's wedding in Indonesia. I made it there and back unscathed. Gradually my world has opened up and expanded as I no longer live in a total state of fear or anxiety and remain committed to living my best life for me and for Grace. I accept that with every month that passes my chances of giving birth to my own baby are less likely, but still, miracles do happen; don't they?

Ultimately, I believe the key to our own happiness always lies within and being a whole-hearted human being means being open to every experience life wants to throw at us including death. None of us are immune from grief or loss, it is the only certainty in life that every living thing must come to an end. I choose not to be defined by my miscarriage; losing Grace is a significant part of my own life story, but it's not all of me. There was life before and now there is a different life after.

As I write this final chapter today is Grace's third birthday. I use the present tense as she is not left behind in the past. She is very much of the now. On her due date birthday in June, it is a day set aside for quiet contemplation, this will always be our special day. Had she been born we would be celebrating her third birthday and so next to me on my desk are three heart shaped candles, lit especially for her. Sitting alongside the candles are the rose quartz angel, my Grace stone and an 'Amazing Grace' rose from the garden. All precious gifts we received for Grace. My husband and I have a moment of reflection together and enjoy a slice of angel cake with our afternoon tea in loving memory of our girl. Her presence is always felt and acknowledged. One of my friends, who sadly lost her baby boy, sent me the most beautiful photo of the name Grace spelled out in stones alongside a stunning river, she thought I may like it. Not only do I like it, I love it; so much so it is now also added to my collection of treasures for Grace in my office where I write.

My heart and soul continue to ache for her; I still wonder about how she would be as a person and what she would look like and how her personality could have developed. The answers to my questions will never come as life continues to roll on without her. What I find comforting is knowing that we have a beautiful connection to Grace. I don't know where she is. But all I know is she is here, in and around me and lives in my heart. She regularly visits us, often unexpectedly, and finds a way to show up especially for special family events and birthdays. This year for my birthday we were in Northumberland and as I waited for my husband to catch me up, I found myself standing right outside a jeweller with a huge 'Grace' sign in the window. 'Did you see what is behind you?' my husband asked. I hadn't noticed until he pointed it out, but I instinctively knew Grace was there.

Music seems to be an excellent on-going communication tool as for my birthday last year I turned on the radio, as the Eurythmics 'Must be talking to an angel' played. Next up was Paul Simon 'Graceland' and finally I heard Guns and Roses with 'Sweet child of mine' - all songs that I know were nudges from Grace appearing one after another. Then on my husband's birthday as I picked him up from the train station and he got into the car yet again 'Graceland' by Paul Simon began to play on the car radio. A favourite I hear frequently is 'It's not over yet' by Grace and as my husband and I were talking about me including the obvious divine timing of the songs that always play when we needed to hear them in the book – 'Nina Simone – My baby just cares for me' began to play. We both laughed and said in unison: 'Grace is here again'.

Recently it was my mum's 70th birthday and we held a family afternoon tea party especially for her at Rosewood House. As I prepared the sandwiches in the kitchen I turned on the radio just as a 'pause for thought' section by the Bishop of Leeds began entitled Amazing Grace. I stopped and listened as the Bishop shared more about his own interpretation of Amazing Grace –

'Grace is an experience of generosity and joy despite the rubbish in life.
Grace speaks of forgiveness and freedom, love and mercy.
Grace breaks the bonds of fear and shines the light in to the darkness of love.
This is Amazing Grace – as slightly interesting Grace would never have worked would it?'

Most definitely not.

As my husband walked into the kitchen he found me in tears whilst attempting to finish making the sandwiches - Grace was not going to miss out on sending her own special birthday message for my mum. The roses from the garden also made an appearance, the 'Grace Rose' and 'Amazing Grace' roses were in bloom and were added to the floral table display and joined us all in the celebrations.

What I didn't expect to discover since we lost her is that through my own grief and suffering I've been led towards rebuilding and transforming myself and my life with grace. Not only with the spirit of Grace Rose but to truly learn how to live with grace in every sense. This is what I mean when I refer to my own *Graceful Awakening.*

Losing Grace shattered my heart and broke me open as a human being and a woman. The person I once was is no more, part of me departed and died with Grace in November 2015 and never returned. Through the trauma and heartache of my miscarriage with Grace it led me to rebuild my life and discover and embrace a more soulful awakened woman who is deeply connected to herself, her powerful inner flame, her intuitive divine feminine spirit and to mother earth, more than ever before. This woman is me.

I've had to do the deep inner healing work to find out who I really am, what I really want for the rest of my days and why, as an awakened and whole woman in her own right. I feel more compassion and empathy towards myself and others as it's been quite a journey through the depths of grief and healing.

Being able to find inner strength and courage to speak the unspeakable, transforms it and as a result releases its grip and power over us. In life there is so much we cannot know, see or understand that occurs for our highest good. Eventually we find our way to reach acceptance of the mystery that surrounds us and let go and release the yesterdays and approach each brand-new day as an opportunity to start over. We can become leaders of our own lives; our wounds are not worn as a badge of honour but become part of who we are. They can propel us forwards so that we become more compassionate, caring, trusting and filled with grace.

Three years after we lost Grace I experienced a powerful past life regression that took me back into another life that was vivid and left a profound impact. Somehow I witnessed myself living another life during the mid-18th century, in poverty stricken London. My life was not a happy one and I saw out my days in a workhouse in London. Throughout my time there I recalled being surrounded by a group of women. I would take new arrivals under my wing, share my insights and wisdom with them and find a way to bring groups of women together and urge them to speak out about the mistreatment and oppression we received by the men-in-suits. I fought against these men seeking change until my dying day. What quickly became transparent is that this trait has followed me through to this lifetime.

It's clearly in my soul and destiny to use my voice, tell my stories and empower other women to do the same. This past life experience re-affirmed something deep within that reassured me that I am on the path I am meant to be on now. This is my destiny. It was powerful and demonstrated that we are here for a reason, we may never know what that is, but we grow and transform regardless, from all of our lifetime's experiences. Incidentally I was also a mother to five children in that particular lifetime, whilst in the regression I could sense and feel the love my children and I shared. It was exactly the same familiar love I feel between Grace and I and brought me a great feeling of peace and comfort.

Coming back to the here and now I understand that the sacred shows up when you awaken and it has led me towards Grace. The word grace has many meanings and interpretations, it is used for religious and spiritual practices and purposes and I've since found my own interpretation, understanding and wisdom. As I listened to the 'pause for thought' on my mum's birthday I knew that this is how my story ends.

Now I choose to live and work in a state of grace and accept the intuitive guidance and insights I receive in order to live my best life for the both of us. Through my work, speaking and writing I serve others with ease, joy and grace.

Now I see and feel grace everywhere and notice the beauty that surrounds me in nature. Mother earth is always guiding us to notice and pay attention and act on the whispers we receive.

Now I believe in divine love thanks to the connection I have with Grace, I know our bond is an infinite graceful love that can never be lost.

Regardless of how little time we spend with our longed-for babies each and every one brings us something precious and now we have the gift of living with Grace. Our amazing angel Grace Rose transformed everything.

TRANSFORMATION

And so this is what it means to me on how to live with Amazing Grace.

Grace is going with the flow and surrendering.
Grace is gratitude.
Grace is the gift of being in harmony with all that is.
Grace is beauty within and around.
Grace is liberation and freedom.
Grace gives hope, encouragement and courage.
Grace is a process of awakening and enlightenment.
Grace awakens compassion and kindness.
Grace is the catalyst for growth and transformation.
Grace is a way to live.
Grace is divine and infinite love.
Happiness is the spiritual experience of living every minute
with love, gratitude and Grace.
The power of Divine Grace is right here within us all.

\-   Melanie Mackie

RESOURCES

Charities and organisations doing wonderful work to support parents-to-be and research into baby loss:

Baby Loss Awareness Week
babyloss-awareness.org

Genesis Trust
genesisresearchtrust.com

Miscarriage Association
www.miscarriageassociation.org.uk

Saying Goodbye
www.sayinggoodbye.org

Tommy's
www.tommys.org

Holistic Therapies I found beneficial for grief and healing:

Tara Brach Ph.D, Psychologist, Author and Teacher of Meditation, Emotional Healing and Spiritual Awakening.
www.tarabrach.com

Elizabeth Courtis – Marlow Homeopathy
www.marlowhomeopathy.com

Hayley Felton – Healing & Soul Plan Reading
www.hayleyfelton.co.uk

Kristen Neff Ph.D - Pioneering Self-Compassion Researcher, Author and Teacher.
self-compassion.org

Denise O'Dwyer – Past Life Regression
www.fengshuielement.co.uk

Sandy Robson – Hypnotherapy, Psychotherapy, NLP, EMDR and Reprocessing) and Havening (trauma release).
www.sandyrobsonhypnotherapy.co.uk

Jo Tocher – Life After Miscarriage Coaching
life-after-miscarriage.com

Heidi Wells - Emotional Detox Coach, Accredited EFT Practitioner, Intuitive Consultant & Mindfulness Teacher
heidiwells.com

Recommended reading:

Sunshine After the Storm: A Survival Guide for the Grieving Mother by Alexa H Bigwarfe - *Alexa Bigwharfe & Kat Biggie Press 2013*

Rising Strong by Brene Brown – *Vermillion 2015*

The Artist's Way by Julia Cameron – *Pan Books 1993*

Broken Open: How difficult times can help us grow by Elizabeth Lesser - *Random House 2004*

Spirit Babies – How to communicate with the child you were meant to have by Walter Makichen – *Random House 2005*

Womb Wisdom: Awakening the Creative and Forgotten Powers of the Feminine by Padma Aon Prakasha, Anaiya Aon Prakasha - *Inner Traditions International; 2011*

Finding Joy Beyond Childlessness by Lesley Pyne *2018*

Grief Works by Julia Samuel – *Penguin Life 2017*

A Mind of Your Own by Betty Shine – *Harper Collins 1998*

Life After Miscarriage: Your guide to healing after pregnancy loss by Jo Tocher *2018*

Research:

British Medical Journal: Post-traumatic stress, anxiety and depression following miscarriage or ectopic pregnancy: a prospective cohort study – *by Jessica Farren, Maria Jalmbrant, Lieveke Ameye, Karen Joash, Nicola Mitchell-Jones, Sophie Tapp, Dirk Timmerman, Tom Bourne*

http://bmjopen.bmj.com/content/6/11/e011864

GRATITUDE

To all the courageous and brave women who have also lost their own babies – thank you for sharing your own stories and insights with me. Together, collectively we are the change because all of our babies matter.

To Anne Thorn thank you for challenging me to make this book the best it could be and to become a better writer with your brilliant copy-editing. I believe fate, Grace and Toby brought us together.

To all the fabulous women I have had the privilege to work with individually or within the Social Collective. May you continue to be who you really are, show up and speak your truths with authenticity and bravery. Our time is now.

To Hayley Felton thank you for coming into my life and showing me life had another plan for me. In you I have found a kindred spirit and friend - I believe our paths were destined to cross.

To Lesley Pyne thank you for all your guidance, insights and the wonderful conversations. I feel we belong.

To Claire Stallwood thank you for being my friend, for always remembering Grace and for showing up unannounced when I desperately needed you. I will never forget all your love and kindness.

To Ruby also known as the 'Angel in the supermarket' thank you for sharing your struggle with me and inspiring me to be courageous and speak my own truth. I wish for your freedom and a beautiful future for both you and your daughter.

To my beloved Nanny Dorothy, Nanny Elsie and Auntie May. The three incredible women who shaped me as a young girl and woman. You continue to be an endless source of admiration, are loved and will continue to be held in my heart forever.

To my nephews and nieces Orlando, Marissa, Jack, Emily, Silvana and Henry. Miraculous souls who light up our lives – I am extremely proud and honoured to be your Auntie Mel. May your lives be blessed with light, love and adventures. Always live your lives to the fullest and remember to reach for your dreams with Grace.

My family is my world so thank you to my Dad, Mum and sister Carla. The Tooley's always rock!

To my magnificent Uncle Ray who encouraged me to be brave and keep on writing to tell our story. Thank you.

To my in-laws Jan and Mick and for another very special angel, Caroline. Never forgotten, always remembered.

And an enormous thank you to my brother-in-law

Wayne for all his fund-raising and bike-riding efforts for Tommy's.

The loving bond I have with my own mum is one I could have only wished for with my children. My mumma Lesley is always by my side encouraging me forwards and believed in me when I no longer believed in myself. I doubt I would have continued to write this book let alone finish it without her. Thank you for being my mum, answering my endless questions about our female ancestral history, reading and re-reading my manuscript and always remembering Grace Rose along with me.

Finally, to my husband Darrin from the moment we met I knew we were destined to be together. There is no one else on earth I'd rather have journeyed through my life with. Thank you for trusting and believing in me to write our story and for always encouraging me to be who I really am. You are my bestest – with all my love forever and always xxx

ABOUT THE AUTHOR

Melanie Mackie is a writer, an explorer, nature lover, spiritual hippie, a bit of a creative and an avid gardener. She currently lives to the west of London near the River Thames, with her beloved husband and Monkey Mogs Billy and Lola.

In 2015 Melanie lost her longed-for baby Grace Rose during her pregnancy. This heart-breaking loss was a catalyst to changing her entire life. Eventually she chose the light and committed to living her best life, for her and especially for Grace.

Melanie also runs her own award-winning mentoring business and is an Intuitive Mentor and Consultant. She has worked with female entrepreneurs all over the globe since 2009 and encourages and empowers her clients to put themselves at the forefront of their lives, work and businesses so that they experience remarkable personal growth, deep transformation and awaken to a new way of being and doing.

Melanie is a speaker and her talks raise awareness of the impact of miscarriage, grief, healing and the power of our divine feminine wisdom. All subjects that have been hidden, buried and silenced for far too long.

To find out more visit melaniemackie.org

30929820R00106

Printed in Great
Britain
by Amazon